easy **world** craft

Crochet

easy world craft

Crochet

A handy step-by-step guide

DK | Penguin Random House

Project Editor Katharine Goddard
Senior Art Editors Glenda Fisher, Elaine Hewson
Managing Editor Penny Smith
Senior Managing Art Editor Marianne Markham
Jacket Creative Nicola Powling
Pre-Production Producer Rebecca Fallowfield
Senior Producer Charlotte Oliver
Art Director Jane Bull
Publisher Mary Ling
Special Sales Creative Project Manager Alison Donovan

DK INDIA
Managing Editor Alicia Ingty
Editors Janashree Singha, Manasvi Vohra
Senior Art Editor Balwant Singh
Art Editor Vandna Sonkariya
Assistant Art Editor Nikita Sodhi
Managing Art Editor Navidita Thapa
Pre-Production Manager Sunil Sharma
DTP Designers Satish Chandra Gaur, Rajdeep Singh

First published in Great Britain in 2014
by Dorling Kindersley Limited
80 Strand, London WC2R 0RL

Material in this publication was previously published in:
The Needlecraft Book (2010), Crochet Step by Step (2013)

A CIP catalogue record for this book is available
from the British Library
ISBN 978-1-4093-6926-4

Printed and bound in China

All images © Dorling Kindersley Limited
For further information see: **www.dkimages.com**

A WORLD OF IDEAS
SEE ALL THERE IS TO KNOW

CONTENTS

INTRODUCTION

This book is suitable for readers with no previous experience of crochet, as well as for crocheters hoping to improve their technique. It will also serve as an excellent reference for anyone with more advanced skills. *Crochet* guides you through basic techniques and stitches, covering the relevant abbreviations and symbols on the way.

If you're new to crochet, start by familiarizing yourself with the tools and materials. The pages that follow ease you into the essential skills you will need. For example, in the Techniques section, you will learn how to hold the yarn and hook, how to make a slip knot and how to create a foundation chain. You will then be taken through the most common crochet stitches as well as the "ins-and-outs" of reading crochet patterns. Once you've mastered these basics, you are free to move through the sections, refining your skills, and practising the techniques that you enjoy the most. A section of beautiful projects to make will inspire you to put your newly honed skills to the test, with the added knowledge of how to finish your item by attaching hooks, eyes, and buttons.

TOOLS AND MATERIALS

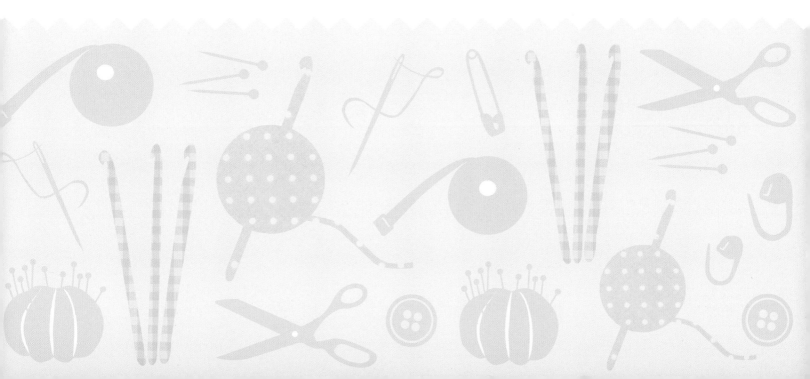

TOOLS AND MATERIALS

To get started with crochet, have a look first at the wonderful variety of yarns available. Crochet can be used to create an astounding range of textiles, from sturdy textures suitable for coats to graceful, alluring lace. It requires very little equipment, so is probably the most economical needlework craft.

YARNS	Any yarn can usually be crocheted into an attractive textile using a small range of hook sizes, each of which produces a slightly looser or slightly tighter fabric that holds its shape well.

SMOOTH WOOL YARNS

≪ WOOL YARN WEIGHTS
Super-fine, fine, and lightweight wool yarns work best for crochet garments; the thicker yarns are only suitable for blankets. (A full explanation of yarn weights is given on page 13.)

SYNTHETIC YARNS
Many synthetic fibre yarns or synthetic and natural fibre mixes are very good imitations of pure wool. So if you are looking for a less expensive alternative to wool, try some of these out. They do not age as well as wool, but they are easy to care for.

SMOOTH COTTON YARNS

FINE-WEIGHT COTTON YARNS ≫
This thicker yarn is a good weight for garments and accessories and will show the texture of stitch patterns clearly.

COTTON CROCHET THREADS ≫
Traditionally, crochet was worked in cotton threads that were suitable for lace. Today cotton threads are still used for lace edgings and filet crochet (see pages 54–55 and pages 38–39).

MULTICOLOURED YARNS

"SOCK" YARN
"Sock" yarn is a spaced-dyed yarn originally designed for knitting socks – as the sock is knitted the yarn changes colour along its length and forms patterns. The fine-weight versions of this type of multicoloured yarn can be used for crochet as well, to produce interesting effects.

‹‹ VARIEGATED YARN
Yarns flecked with different colours or dyed different colours along the length of one strand are useful for achieving multicoloured effects without needing to change yarn or colours.

TEXTURED AND NOVELTY YARNS

‹‹ METALLIC THREAD
A fine, metallic thread is ideally suited to openwork crochet for evening shawls and scarves.

FINE MOHAIR YARN ››
This textured yarn will produce a tactile crocheted piece, partially obscuring the stitches.

TEXTURED NOVELTY YARNS
Highly textured yarns, such as bouclés and shaggy "fur" yarns are difficult to crochet with, so stick to simple double crochet when using them. They obscure the crochet stitches and produce an allover textured-effect fabric.

UNUSUAL YARNS

‹‹ COLOURED WIRE
Thin 0.3mm (28 gauge) wire is flexible enough to work in crochet for jewellery.

STRING ››
Ideal for crocheting bags and containers, string is available in many colours and thicknesses.

FABRIC STRIPS ⌃
Fabric strips can be crocheted to produce household items and accessories.

‹‹ STRIPS CUT FROM PLASTIC BAGS
Crochet works well with unusual materials, such as strips of plastic, for making items with simple double crochet stitches.

YARN
PUT-UPS

A yarn "put-up" is a specific quantity of yarn packaged for sale. The most common put-ups for yarns are balls, hanks, and skeins. You can also buy bigger put-ups in cones, although these are more commonly sold for machine knitting than for crochet.

DONUTS
The stock in a yarn store may include balls that look like "donuts". These are ready to use: just pull the yarn from the centre to start crocheting.

BALLS
One of the most common put-ups, balls of yarn are ready to use. Keep the label in place to ensure that the yarn doesn't unravel as you work.

HANKS
A hank, or skein, is a twisted ring of yarn that needs to be wound into a ball before it can be used.

CONES
Cones of yarn are often too heavy to carry around in your craft bag and are best wound into small balls before you start crocheting.

YARN
LABELS

Yarn put-ups are most commonly packaged with a label that provides you with all the information you need to crochet successfully. Before you buy, always read the label carefully to establish the type of yarn, suggested hook size, care instructions, and ball length.

READING A YARN LABEL »
Decide whether you require an easy-care yarn and check the care instructions. Fibre content will indicate whether the yarn is synthetic or a synthetic mix, or 100 per cent natural, each giving a different effect as it ages. The ball length will enable you to calculate how many balls are required when you are substituting yarn (see opposite page). Check the dye-lot number if you are purchasing several balls, as variations in colour can occur across different dye-lots.

Natural or synthetic fibres or a mix of both

When buying a substitute yarn, decide how much you need by ball length rather than ball weight

COLOUR NAME/NUMBER

DYE-LOT NUMBER

Manufacturer's name

YARN NAME
Fibre content

GENERIC YARN WEIGHT

Ball weight in g/oz
Ball length in metres/yards

SUGGESTED TENSION
and needle/hook size

Care instructions

Buy all balls from the same dye-lot

See next page for explanation of yarn weights

Indicates the recommended hook size and the resulting tension

Whether hand washable, machine washable, or dry cleanable

YARN WEIGHTS

• **The yarn "weight"** refers to the thickness of a yarn. Some yarns are spun by manufacturers to fall into what are considered as "standard" yarn weights, such as US sport or worsted and UK double-knitting and aran. These standard weights have long histories and will probably be around for some time to come. However, even within these "standard" weights there is slight variation in thickness, and textured novelty yarns are not easy to categorize by thickness alone.

• **Visual yarn thickness** is only one indicator of a yarn-weight category. A yarn can look thicker than another yarn purely because of its loft, the air between the fibres, and the springiness of the strands. By pulling a strand between your two hands you can see how much it has by how much the thickness diminishes when the yarn is stretched. The ply is not an indication of yarn thickness.

Plies are the strands spun together around each other to form the yarn. A yarn with four plies can be very thick or very thin depending on the thickness of each individual ply.

• **In order to help crocheters** attempting to match like for like when looking for a substitute yarn for their pattern, the Craft Yarn Council of America has devised a table of yarn weights. This table (below) demonstrates how to find the perfect yarn substitute if you are unable to purchase the yarn specified in a crochet pattern. The very best indication of a yarn weight is the manufacturer's recommended tension and hook size for the yarn. (These recommendation will produce a fabric that is loose enough to be soft and flexible but not so loose that it loses its shape.) Two yarns with the same fibre content and the same recommended tension and hook size will be perfect substitutes for each other.

STANDARD YARN-WEIGHT SYSTEM

YARN WEIGHT SYMBOL & CATEGORY NAMES	0 LACE	1 SUPER FINE	2 FINE	3 LIGHT	4 MEDIUM	5 BULKY	6 SUPER BULKY
Types of yarns in category	Fingering, 10-count crochet thread	Sock, baby, fingering, UK "4-ply"	Sport, baby	Double knitting, light worsted	Worsted, afghan, aran	Chunky, craft, rug	Bulky, roving
Crochet tension ranges in dc to 10cm/4in	32–42 trebles	21–32 sts	16–20 sts	12–17 sts	11–14 sts	8–11 sts	5–9 sts
Recommended hook in metric size range	1.6–2.25mm	2.25–3.5mm	3.5–4.5mm	4.5–5.5mm	5.5–6.5mm	6.5–9mm	9mm and larger
Recommended hook in US size range	6 steel, 7 steel, 8 steel, B-1	B-1 to E-4	E-4 to 7	7 to I-9	I-9 to K-10½	K-10½ to M-13	M-13 and larger

GUIDELINES ONLY The above reflect the most commonly used tensions and hook sizes for specific yarn categories. The categories of yarn, tension ranges, and recommended hook sizes have been devised by the Craft Yarn Council of America (YarnStandards.com).

4mm (UK 8/ US G-6)

Recommended crochet hook size

Tension over a 10cm (4in) test square

SHADE/ COLOUR

520

Shade/colour number

DYE LOT NUMBER

313

Dye lot number

50g

NETT AT STANDARD CONDITION IN ACCORDANCE WITH BS984

Weight of ball or skein

100% WOOL

Fibre content

CROCHET
HOOKS

If you are a beginner, start learning to crochet with a good-quality standard metal crochet hook. Once you know how to work the basic stitches with a lightweight wool yarn and a 4.5mm (US size 7) hook, branch out and try some other types of hooks in order to find the one that suits you best.

STANDARD METAL HOOK

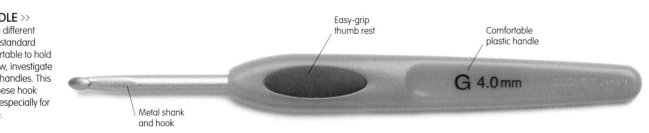

Hook tip

Throat

Hook lip

Shank

Thumb rest

Handle

PARTS OF A CROCHET HOOK ⩔
The hook lip grabs the yarn to form the loops and the shank determines the size of the loop. The crochet handle gives weight to the tool and enhances a good grip.

ALTERNATIVE HOOK HANDLES

COMFORT HANDLE ≫
Hook handles come in different shapes. If you find the standard crochet hook uncomfortable to hold because it is too narrow, investigate hooks with alternative handles. This is a high-quality Japanese hook designed and refined especially for comfort and good grip.

Easy-grip thumb rest

Comfortable plastic handle

G 4.0 mm

Metal shank and hook

HOOK TYPES

Point protector

⫶⫶ LACE HOOK
Because lace crochet hooks are so fine, ranging from 0.6mm (US size 14 steel) to 1.75mm (US size 5 steel), they are always manufactured in metal. Keep them with their metal point protectors in place to avoid accidents.

⫶⫶ METAL HOOKS
Some ranges of aluminium hooks are available in bright colours – a different colour for each size, which is handy for picking up the right size at a glance.

⫶⫶ WOODEN HOOKS
Hardwood and bamboo hooks are very attractive and lighter in weight than metal hooks. They also provide a good grip to prevent your fingers slipping when crocheting.

⫶⫶ PLASTIC HOOKS
Plastic hooks are not as precisely made as metal and wooden hooks, but they come in great colours, so are enjoyable to work with.

JUMBO HOOKS ⩔
The largest crochet hook sizes – from a 10mm (US size N-15) to a 20mm (US size S) are made in plastic. They are used for making thick crochet fabric very quickly.

HOOK SIZES

Crochet hooks are manufactured in the various sizes (diameters) listed in the hook conversion chart on the opposite page. The millimetre sizes are the diameters of the hook shank, which determines the size of the crochet stitches.

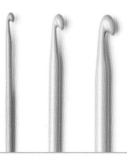

Although the middle range of hook sizes – from 2mm (US size B-1) to 9mm (US size M-13) – are the most commonly used, the finer and thicker hooks are also very popular for lace crochet and jumbo crochet. See page 15 for which hook size to use with the different yarn weights.

CONVERSION CHART

This chart gives the conversions between the various hook-size systems. Where there are no exact conversions possible the nearest equivalent is given.

EU METRIC	US SIZES	OLD UK
0.6mm	14 steel	
0.75mm	12 steel	
1mm	11 steel	
1.25mm	7 steel	
1.5mm	6 steel	
1.75mm	5 steel	
2mm		14
2.25mm	B-1	
2.5mm		12
2.75mm	C-2	
3mm		10
3.25mm	D-3	
3.5mm	E-4	9
3.75mm	F-5	
4mm	G-6	8
4.5mm	7	7
5mm	H-8	6
5.5mm	I-9	5
6mm	J-10	4
6.5mm	K-10½	3
7mm		2
8mm	L-11	
9mm	M-13	
10mm	N-15	
12mm	P	
15mm	Q (16mm)	
20mm	S (19mm)	

OTHER EQUIPMENT

To get started you only need a crochet hook and a blunt-ended yarn needle. You may have some of the other essentials in your sewing kit already.

THE ESSENTIALS

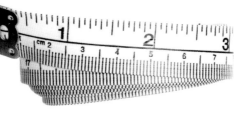

TAPE MEASURE ☆
Keep a tape measure to hand for checking your tension and measuring your crochet.

PINS ☆
Use pins with glass heads or large heads (such as knitting pins), for seams and blocking (see page 50).

SCISSORS ☆
Keep a sharp pair of scissors on hand for cutting off yarn and trimming off yarn ends.

BLUNT-ENDED YARN NEEDLES ☆
Use these for sewing seams and darning in yarn ends (make sure the needle has a big enough eye for your chosen yarn).

HANDY EXTRAS

STITCH MARKERS ☆
These can be hooked onto the crochet to mark a specific row or a specific stitch in the row, or to mark the right-side of your crochet.

ROW COUNTER ☆
These are useful for keeping track of where you are in your crochet. String on a length of cotton yarn and hang it around your neck – change it each time you complete a row.

YARN BOBBINS ☆
Useful for holding short lengths of yarn for jacquard crochet.

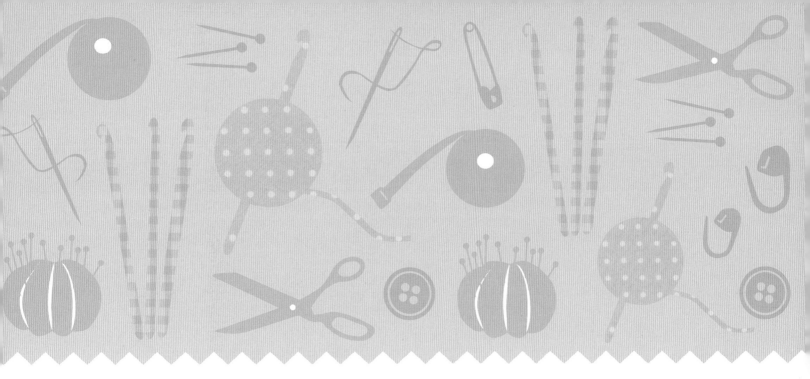

TECHNIQUES

BASIC STITCHES

Learning to crochet takes a little longer than learning to knit because there are several basic stitches to master. But there is no need to learn all the stitches at once. With only chain stitches and double crochet at your disposal, you can make attractive striped blankets and cushion covers in luscious yarns.

GETTING STARTED	Before making your first loop, the slip knot (see opposite page), get to know your hook and how to hold it. First, review the detailed explanation of the parts of the hook on page 14. Then try out the various hook- and yarn-holding techniques below when learning how to make chain stitches. If you ever learned crochet as a child, you will automatically hold the hook the way you originally learned to, and you should stick to this whether it is the pencil or knife position.

HOLDING THE HOOK

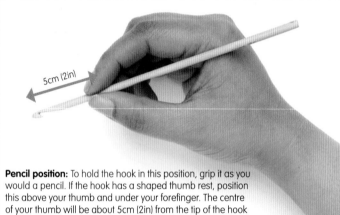

5cm (2in)

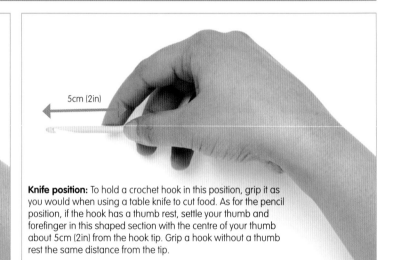

5cm (2in)

Pencil position: To hold the hook in this position, grip it as you would a pencil. If the hook has a shaped thumb rest, position this above your thumb and under your forefinger. The centre of your thumb will be about 5cm (2in) from the tip of the hook if the hook has a thumb rest, and this is where you should also hold a hook without a thumb rest.

Knife position: To hold a crochet hook in this position, grip it as you would when using a table knife to cut food. As for the pencil position, if the hook has a thumb rest, settle your thumb and forefinger in this shaped section with the centre of your thumb about 5cm (2in) from the hook tip. Grip a hook without a thumb rest the same distance from the tip.

HOLDING THE YARN

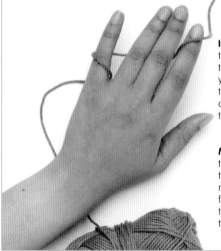

In order to control the flow of the yarn to your hook, you need to lace it around the fingers of your free hand. Both of the techniques shown here are only suggestions, so feel free to develop your own.

Method one: Start by winding the yarn around your little finger, then pass it under your two middle fingers and over your forefinger. With this method the forefinger is used to position the yarn.

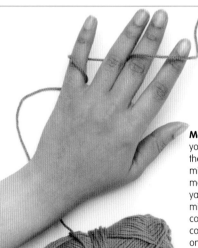

Method two: Wrap the yarn around your little finger, then pass it behind the next finger and over the top of the middle finger and forefinger. This method allows you to position the yarn with either the forefinger or middle finger, whichever is more comfortable and gives you more control (see Tensioning Your Yarn on the opposite page).

MAKING A SLIP KNOT

1 To make the first loop (called the slip knot) on your needle, begin by crossing the yarn coming from the ball over the yarn end (called the yarn tail) to form a circle of yarn.

Yarn coming from ball

Yarn tail

2 Insert the tip of the hook through the circle of yarn.

3 Then use the hook to grab the ball end of the yarn and pull the yarn through the circle.

4 This forms a loop on the hook and a loose, open knot below the loop.

5 Pull both ends of the yarn firmly to tighten the knot and the loop around the shank of the hook.

6 Make sure the completed slip knot is tight enough on the hook that it won't fall off but not so tight that you can barely slide it along the hook's shank.

Make sure loop is secure but slides easily

Ball end of yarn

7 The yarn tail on the slip knot should be at least 15cm (6in) long so it can be threaded onto a blunt-ended yarn needle and darned in later. However, a crochet pattern may instruct you to leave an extra-long yarn tail (called a long loose end) to use for seams or other purposes.

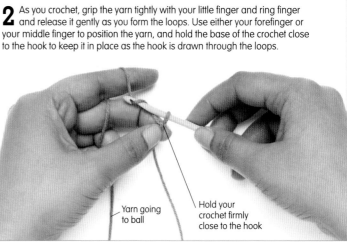

Extra-long yarn tail

TENSIONING YOUR YARN

1 With your slip knot on your hook, try out some yarn holding techniques. Wrap the yarn around your little finger and then lace it through your other fingers as desired, but so that it ends up over the tip of your forefinger (or your forefinger and middle finger).

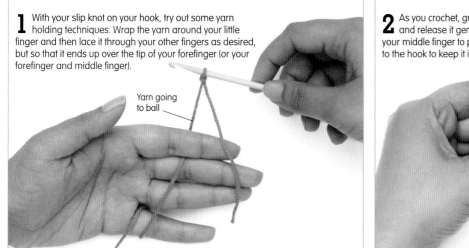

Yarn going to ball

2 As you crochet, grip the yarn tightly with your little finger and ring finger and release it gently as you form the loops. Use either your forefinger or your middle finger to position the yarn, and hold the base of the crochet close to the hook to keep it in place as the hook is drawn through the loops.

Yarn going to ball

Hold your crochet firmly close to the hook

CHAIN STITCHES
Abbreviation = *ch*

Chain stitches are the first crochet stitches you need to learn because they form the base for all other stitches – called a foundation chain. They are used in combination with other basic stitches to create a vast array of crochet stitch patterns, both dense textured stitches and lacy ones. Practise chain stitches until you are comfortable holding a hook and releasing and tensioning yarn.

MAKING A FOUNDATION CHAIN

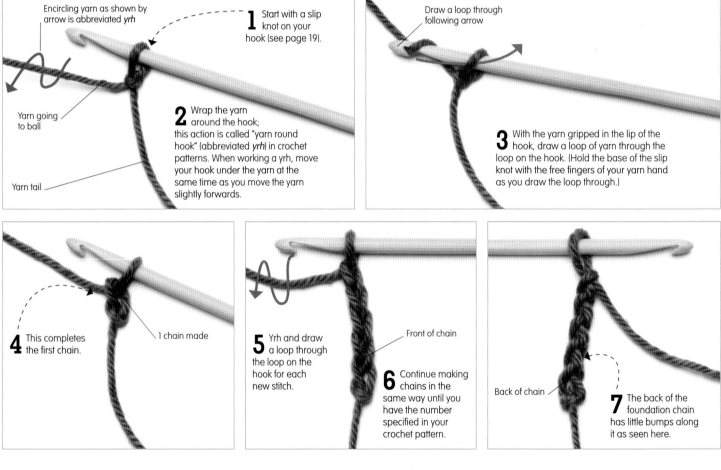

Encircling yarn as shown by arrow is abbreviated *yrh*

Yarn going to ball

Yarn tail

1 Start with a slip knot on your hook (see page 19).

2 Wrap the yarn around the hook; this action is called "yarn round hook" (abbreviated *yrh*) in crochet patterns. When working a yrh, move your hook under the yarn at the same time as you move the yarn slightly forwards.

Draw a loop through following arrow

3 With the yarn gripped in the lip of the hook, draw a loop of yarn through the loop on the hook. (Hold the base of the slip knot with the free fingers of your yarn hand as you draw the loop through.)

4 This completes the first chain.

1 chain made

5 Yrh and draw a loop through the loop on the hook for each new stitch.

Front of chain

6 Continue making chains in the same way until you have the number specified in your crochet pattern.

Back of chain

7 The back of the foundation chain has little bumps along it as seen here.

COUNTING CHAIN STITCHES

Do not count loop on hook

6 | 5 | 4 | 3 | 2 | 1

As you make chains for the foundation chain, count each stitch until you have made the required number. Then before starting your crochet, recount the chains to check that you have the correct number. With the front of the chain facing you, start counting the stitches from the base of the hook and count leftwards.

SIMPLE CHAIN STITCH NECKLACE

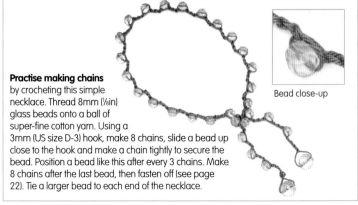

Bead close-up

Practise making chains by crocheting this simple necklace. Thread 8mm (⅛in) glass beads onto a ball of super-fine cotton yarn. Using a 3mm (US size D-3) hook, make 8 chains, slide a bead up close to the hook and make a chain tightly to secure the bead. Position a bead like this after every 3 chains. Make 8 chains after the last bead, then fasten off (see page 22). Tie a larger bead to each end of the necklace.

SLIP STITCH
Abbreviation = ss

Slip stitches are the shortest of all the crochet stitches. Although they can be worked in rows, the resulting fabric is so dense that it is only really suitable for bag handles. However, slip stitches appear very frequently in crochet instructions – to join in new yarn (see page 27), to work invisibly along the top of a row to move to a new position (see page 49), and to join rounds in circular crochet.

WORKING SLIP STITCH AS A FABRIC

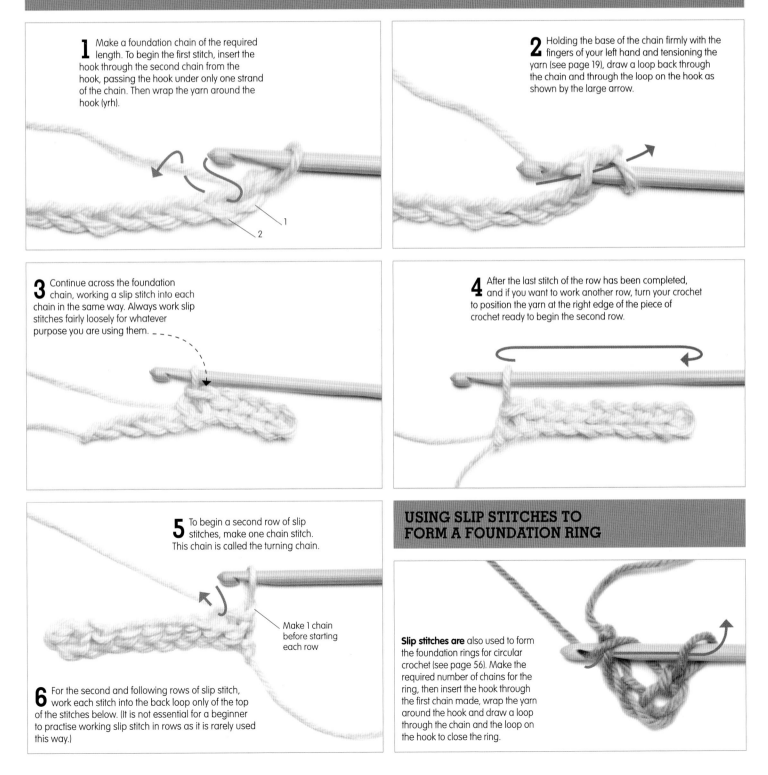

1 Make a foundation chain of the required length. To begin the first stitch, insert the hook through the second chain from the hook, passing the hook under only one strand of the chain. Then wrap the yarn around the hook (yrh).

2 Holding the base of the chain firmly with the fingers of your left hand and tensioning the yarn (see page 19), draw a loop back through the chain and through the loop on the hook as shown by the large arrow.

3 Continue across the foundation chain, working a slip stitch into each chain in the same way. Always work slip stitches fairly loosely for whatever purpose you are using them.

4 After the last stitch of the row has been completed, and if you want to work another row, turn your crochet to position the yarn at the right edge of the piece of crochet ready to begin the second row.

5 To begin a second row of slip stitches, make one chain stitch. This chain is called the turning chain.

Make 1 chain before starting each row

6 For the second and following rows of slip stitch, work each stitch into the back loop only of the top of the stitches below. (It is not essential for a beginner to practise working slip stitch in rows as it is rarely used this way.)

USING SLIP STITCHES TO FORM A FOUNDATION RING

Slip stitches are also used to form the foundation rings for circular crochet (see page 56). Make the required number of chains for the ring, then insert the hook through the first chain made, wrap the yarn around the hook and draw a loop through the chain and the loop on the hook to close the ring.

FASTENING OFF
CHAINS AND SLIP STITCHES

Stopping your crochet when it is complete is called fastening off. As there is only one loop on your hook, the process is extremely simple, much quicker and easier than casting off stitches in knitting! Here is a visual aid for how to fasten off a length of chains or a row of slip stitches. The principle is the same for all stitches.

FASTENING OFF A LENGTH OF CHAINS

1 Remove the loop from the hook.

2 Pull out the loop to enlarge it so that it does not start to unravel.

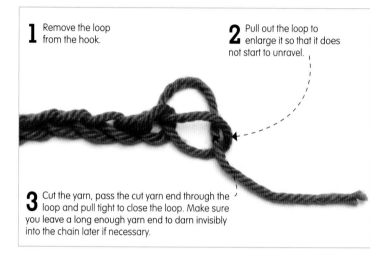

3 Cut the yarn, pass the cut yarn end through the loop and pull tight to close the loop. Make sure you leave a long enough yarn end to darn invisibly into the chain later if necessary.

FASTENING OFF SLIP STITCHES

Fasten off in the same way as for the chain stitches. Alternatively, you can use the hook to draw the cut end through the remaining loop as shown here by the large arrow.

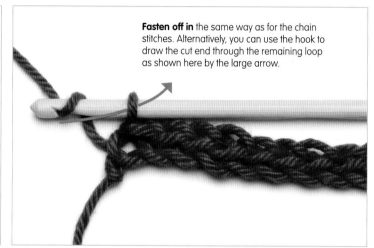

DOUBLE
CROCHET
Abbreviation = *dc*

Double crochet is the easiest crochet stitch to learn and the one crocheters use most frequently, either on its own or in combination with other stitches. Take your time learning and practising the stitch, because once you become proficient in double crochet the taller stitches will be much easier to master. It forms a dense fabric that is suitable for many types of garments and accessories. It is also the stitch used for toys and containers because it can be worked tightly to form a stiff, firm textile.

When double crochet is worked back and forth in rows, it looks identical on both sides. Worked in the round it looks different on the right and wrong sides, which you can see on page 56.

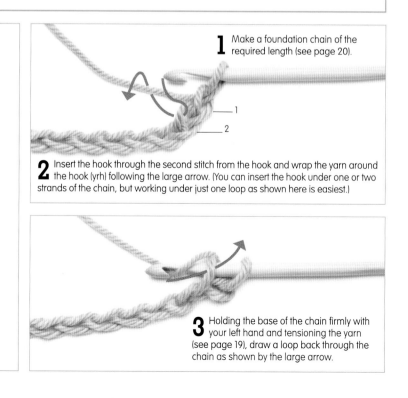

1 Make a foundation chain of the required length (see page 20).

2 Insert the hook through the second stitch from the hook and wrap the yarn around the hook (yrh) following the large arrow. (You can insert the hook under one or two strands of the chain, but working under just one loop as shown here is easiest.)

3 Holding the base of the chain firmly with your left hand and tensioning the yarn (see page 19), draw a loop back through the chain as shown by the large arrow.

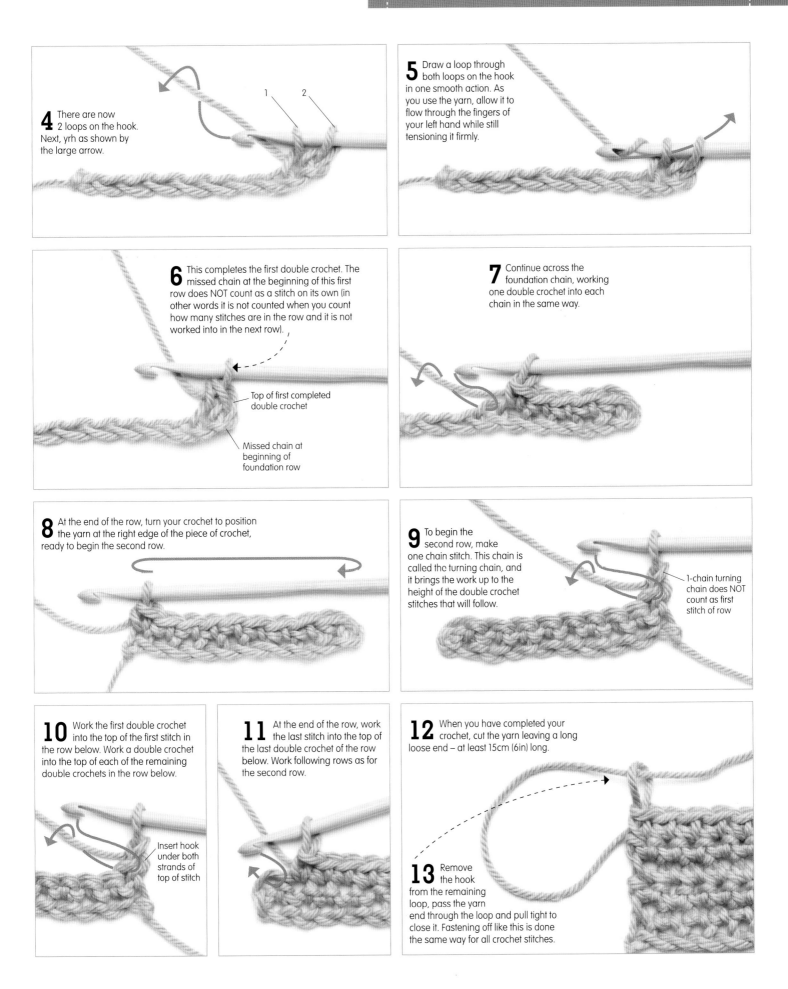

4 There are now 2 loops on the hook. Next, yrh as shown by the large arrow.

1 2

5 Draw a loop through both loops on the hook in one smooth action. As you use the yarn, allow it to flow through the fingers of your left hand while still tensioning it firmly.

6 This completes the first double crochet. The missed chain at the beginning of this first row does NOT count as a stitch on its own (in other words it is not counted when you count how many stitches are in the row and it is not worked into in the next row).

Top of first completed double crochet

Missed chain at beginning of foundation row

7 Continue across the foundation chain, working one double crochet into each chain in the same way.

8 At the end of the row, turn your crochet to position the yarn at the right edge of the piece of crochet, ready to begin the second row.

9 To begin the second row, make one chain stitch. This chain is called the turning chain, and it brings the work up to the height of the double crochet stitches that will follow.

1-chain turning chain does NOT count as first stitch of row

10 Work the first double crochet into the top of the first stitch in the row below. Work a double crochet into the top of each of the remaining double crochets in the row below.

Insert hook under both strands of top of stitch

11 At the end of the row, work the last stitch into the top of the last double crochet of the row below. Work following rows as for the second row.

12 When you have completed your crochet, cut the yarn leaving a long loose end – at least 15cm (6in) long.

13 Remove the hook from the remaining loop, pass the yarn end through the loop and pull tight to close it. Fastening off like this is done the same way for all crochet stitches.

HALF TREBLE
CROCHET
Abbreviation = htr

After slip stitches and double crochet, half treble crochet comes next in order of stitch heights. It is firm like double crochet and fairly dense, but produces a slightly softer texture, which makes it ideal for warm baby garments. Don't attempt to learn how to work half trebles until you make double crochet stitches with confidence.

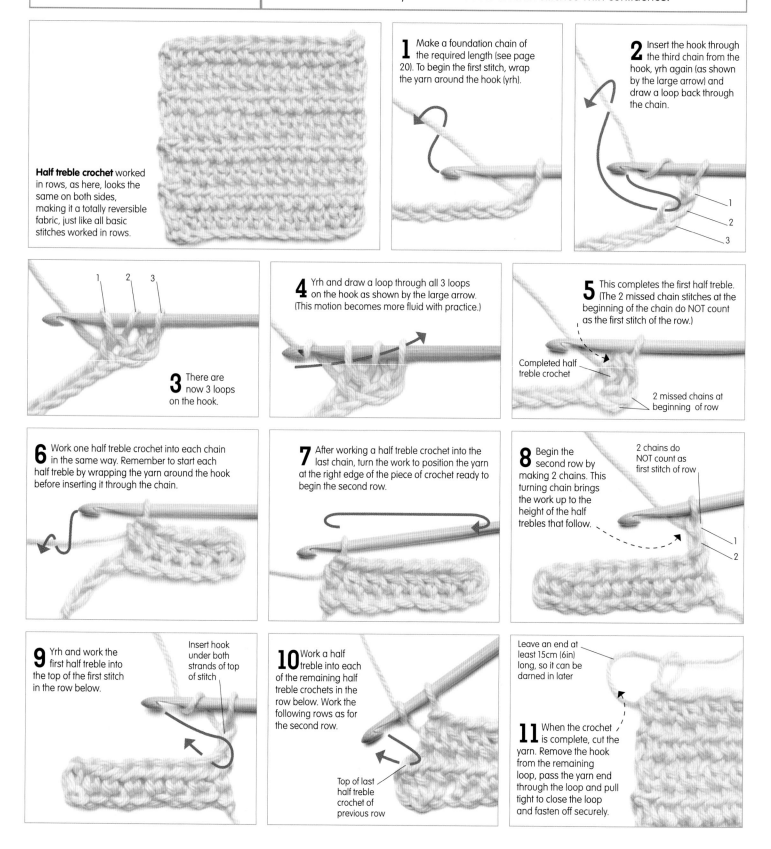

Half treble crochet worked in rows, as here, looks the same on both sides, making it a totally reversible fabric, just like all basic stitches worked in rows.

1 Make a foundation chain of the required length (see page 20). To begin the first stitch, wrap the yarn around the hook (yrh).

2 Insert the hook through the third chain from the hook, yrh again (as shown by the large arrow) and draw a loop back through the chain.

3 There are now 3 loops on the hook.

4 Yrh and draw a loop through all 3 loops on the hook as shown by the large arrow. (This motion becomes more fluid with practice.)

5 This completes the first half treble. (The 2 missed chain stitches at the beginning of the chain do NOT count as the first stitch of the row.)

Completed half treble crochet

2 missed chains at beginning of row

6 Work one half treble crochet into each chain in the same way. Remember to start each half treble by wrapping the yarn around the hook before inserting it through the chain.

7 After working a half treble crochet into the last chain, turn the work to position the yarn at the right edge of the piece of crochet ready to begin the second row.

8 Begin the second row by making 2 chains. This turning chain brings the work up to the height of the half trebles that follow.

2 chains do NOT count as first stitch of row

9 Yrh and work the first half treble into the top of the first stitch in the row below.

Insert hook under both strands of top of stitch

10 Work a half treble into each of the remaining half treble crochets in the row below. Work the following rows as for the second row.

Top of last half treble crochet of previous row

11 When the crochet is complete, cut the yarn. Remove the hook from the remaining loop, pass the yarn end through the loop and pull tight to close the loop and fasten off securely.

Leave an end at least 15cm (6in) long, so it can be darned in later

TREBLE CROCHET
Abbreviation = tr

Treble crochet produces a more open and softer crochet fabric than the denser double and half treble crochet. Because treble crochet is a tall stitch, the fabric grows quickly as you proceed, which makes it the most popular of all crochet stitches.

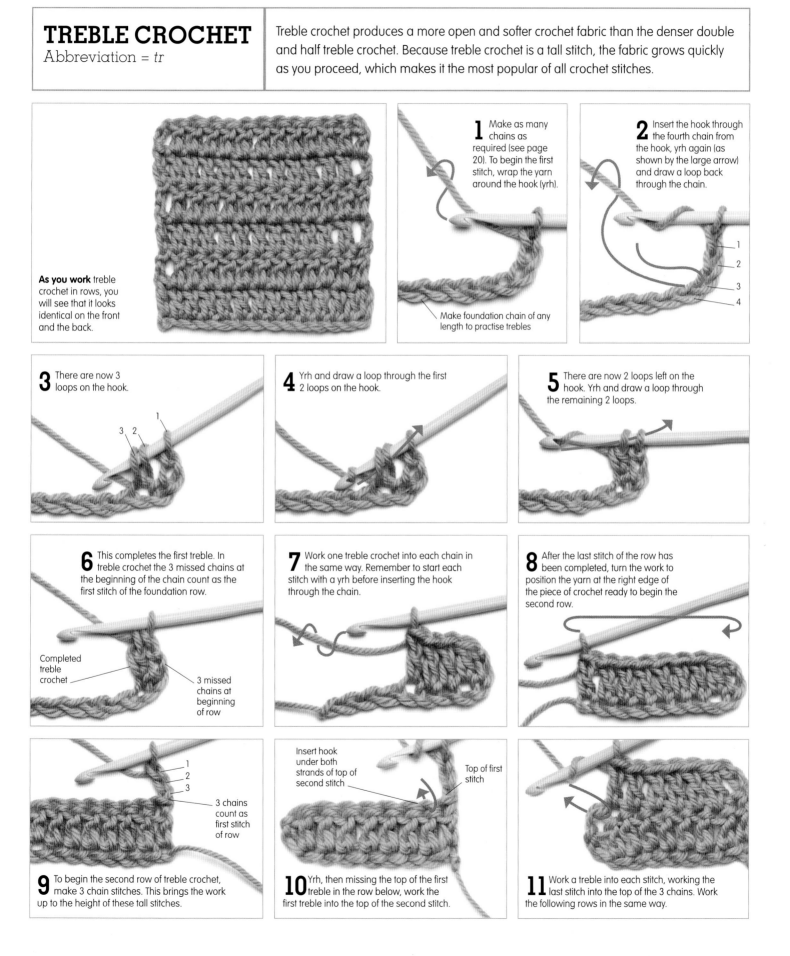

As you work treble crochet in rows, you will see that it looks identical on the front and the back.

1 Make as many chains as required (see page 20). To begin the first stitch, wrap the yarn around the hook (yrh).

Make foundation chain of any length to practise trebles

2 Insert the hook through the fourth chain from the hook, yrh again (as shown by the large arrow) and draw a loop back through the chain.

1
2
3
4

3 There are now 3 loops on the hook.

3 2 1

4 Yrh and draw a loop through the first 2 loops on the hook.

5 There are now 2 loops left on the hook. Yrh and draw a loop through the remaining 2 loops.

6 This completes the first treble. In treble crochet the 3 missed chains at the beginning of the chain count as the first stitch of the foundation row.

Completed treble crochet

3 missed chains at beginning of row

7 Work one treble crochet into each chain in the same way. Remember to start each stitch with a yrh before inserting the hook through the chain.

8 After the last stitch of the row has been completed, turn the work to position the yarn at the right edge of the piece of crochet ready to begin the second row.

9 To begin the second row of treble crochet, make 3 chain stitches. This brings the work up to the height of these tall stitches.

1
2
3
3 chains count as first stitch of row

10 Yrh, then missing the top of the first treble in the row below, work the first treble into the top of the second stitch.

Insert hook under both strands of top of second stitch

Top of first stitch

11 Work a treble into each stitch, working the last stitch into the top of the 3 chains. Work the following rows in the same way.

# DOUBLE TREBLE CROCHET
Abbreviation = *dtr*

Worked in a very similar way to treble crochet, double treble crochet stitches are approximately one chain length taller because the stitch is begun with two wraps instead of only one (see page 28). Double trebles are often used in lace crochet and in crochet motifs.

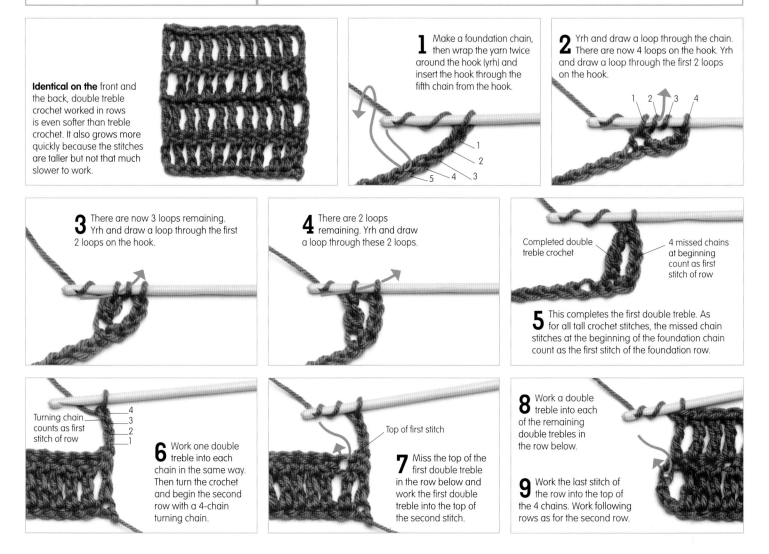

Identical on the front and the back, double treble crochet worked in rows is even softer than treble crochet. It also grows more quickly because the stitches are taller but not that much slower to work.

1 Make a foundation chain, then wrap the yarn twice around the hook (yrh) and insert the hook through the fifth chain from the hook.

2 Yrh and draw a loop through the chain. There are now 4 loops on the hook. Yrh and draw a loop through the first 2 loops on the hook.

3 There are now 3 loops remaining. Yrh and draw a loop through the first 2 loops on the hook.

4 There are 2 loops remaining. Yrh and draw a loop through these 2 loops.

Completed double treble crochet

4 missed chains at beginning count as first stitch of row

5 This completes the first double treble. As for all tall crochet stitches, the missed chain stitches at the beginning of the foundation chain count as the first stitch of the foundation row.

Turning chain counts as first stitch of row

6 Work one double treble into each chain in the same way. Then turn the crochet and begin the second row with a 4-chain turning chain.

Top of first stitch

7 Miss the top of the first double treble in the row below and work the first double treble into the top of the second stitch.

8 Work a double treble into each of the remaining double trebles in the row below.

9 Work the last stitch of the row into the top of the 4 chains. Work following rows as for the second row.

# TRIPLE TREBLE CROCHET
Abbreviation = *trtr*

Stitches taller than double trebles are all worked in the same way as double trebles, except that more wraps are wound around the hook before the stitch is begun and they require taller turning chains. Once you can work triple trebles easily, you will be able to work quadruple and quintuple trebles without much effort.

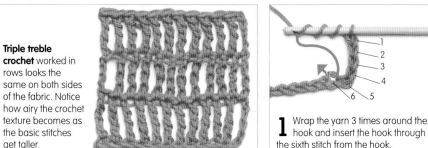

Triple treble crochet worked in rows looks the same on both sides of the fabric. Notice how airy the crochet texture becomes as the basic stitches get taller.

1 Wrap the yarn 3 times around the hook and insert the hook through the sixth stitch from the hook.

5 missed chains count as first stitch of row

2 Work the loops off the hook two at a time as for double trebles. Remember to wrap the yarn three times around the hook before starting each stitch. Start following rows with 5 chains.

BEGINNER'S TIPS

It is important to learn how to count stitches so you can make sure you retain the same number as your crochet grows. Two other essential techniques are how to join in a new ball of yarn and how to darn in yarn ends when your piece of crochet is complete.

COUNTING CROCHET STITCHES

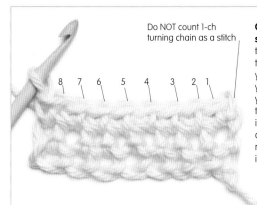

Do NOT count 1-ch turning chain as a stitch

8 7 6 5 4 3 2 1

Counting double crochet stitches: With the front of the last row facing, count the top of each stitch. If you are losing stitches as your crochet grows, then you are probably failing to work into the last stitch in the row below; if you are gaining stitches, you may have worked twice into the same stitch.

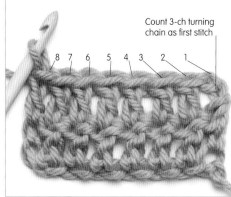

Count 3-ch turning chain as first stitch

8 7 6 5 4 3 2 1

Counting trebles: With the front of the last row facing, count the turning chain as the first stitch, then count the top of each treble. If you are losing stitches as your crochet grows, you are probably failing to work into the top of the turning chain; if you are gaining stitches, you may be working into the first treble of the row, instead of missing it.

JOINING IN NEW YARN

Method one: Always join on a new yarn at the beginning of a row if possible. Simply drop the old yarn and pull the new yarn through the loop on the hook, then begin the row in the usual way. Darn in the yarn ends later.

New yarn

Old yarn

Method two: This method is suitable for both stripes and plain crochet fabrics. First, fasten off the old yarn. Then place a slip knot on the hook, insert the hook through the first stitch of the row and draw a loop through the top of the stitch and the loop on the hook.

New yarn

New slip knot

Old yarn has been fastened off

DARNING IN YARN

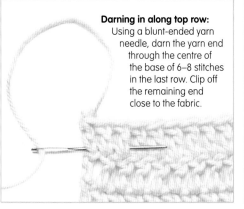

Darning in along top row: Using a blunt-ended yarn needle, darn the yarn end through the centre of the base of 6–8 stitches in the last row. Clip off the remaining end close to the fabric.

Darning in along first row: Using a blunt-ended yarn needle, darn the yarn end through the centre of the base of 6–8 stitches in the first row. Clip off the remaining end close to the fabric.

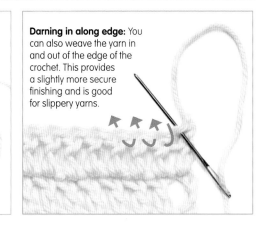

Darning in along edge: You can also weave the yarn in and out of the edge of the crochet. This provides a slightly more secure finishing and is good for slippery yarns.

BASIC STITCHES IN SYMBOLS AND ABBREVIATIONS

Crochet row instructions can be written out with abbreviations or using symbols for the stitches. There is a more detailed explanation for reading stitch pattern instructions on page 32, but directions for the basic stitches are given here in both symbols and abbreviations. This provides an introduction to crochet instructions and a quick reference for how to work crochet fabrics with basic stitches.

STITCH HEIGHTS

The diagram below shows all the basic stitches in symbols and illustrates approximately how tall the stitches are when standing side by side. A double crochet is roughly one chain tall, a half treble crochet two chains tall, a treble crochet three chains tall, and so on. These heights determine the number of turning chains you need to work at the beginning of each row for each of the basic stitches. Also provided here is a reference for which chain to work into when working the first stitch into the foundation chain.

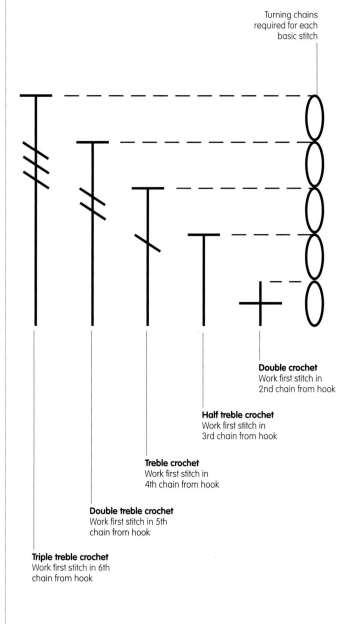

Turning chains required for each basic stitch

Double crochet
Work first stitch in
2nd chain from hook

Half treble crochet
Work first stitch in
3rd chain from hook

Treble crochet
Work first stitch in
4th chain from hook

Double treble crochet
Work first stitch in 5th
chain from hook

Triple treble crochet
Work first stitch in 6th
chain from hook

DOUBLE CROCHET INSTRUCTIONS

Crochet symbol instructions, especially for the basic stitches, are super-easy to understand. Roughly imitating the size and shape of the stitch, the symbols are read from the bottom of the diagram upwards. To get used to very simple crochet instructions, try working double crochet following the written directions and the symbol diagram at the same time (see page 33 for abbreviations list), then try this with the other basic stitches as well.

DOUBLE CROCHET IN ABBREVIATIONS
Make any number of ch.
Row 1 1 dc in 2nd ch from hook, 1 dc in each of rem ch to end, turn.
Row 2 1 ch (does NOT count as a st), 1 dc in each dc to end, turn.
Rep row 2 to form dc fabric.

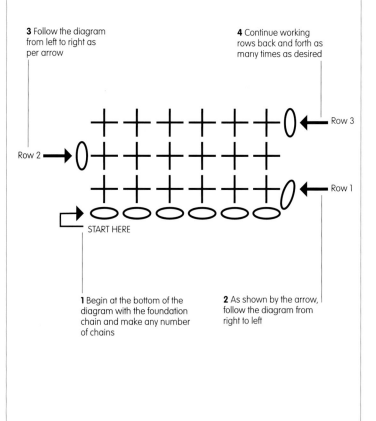

3 Follow the diagram from left to right as per arrow

4 Continue working rows back and forth as many times as desired

Row 3

Row 2

Row 1

START HERE

1 Begin at the bottom of the diagram with the foundation chain and make any number of chains

2 As shown by the arrow, follow the diagram from right to left

HALF TREBLE CROCHET INSTRUCTIONS

The symbol for half treble is a vertical line with a horizontal bar at the top, and it is about twice as tall as the double crochet symbol, just like the stitch is in real life. Read the written instructions for this basic stitch (below) and look at the chart at the same time. The direction of each arrow indicates whether to read the chart from left to right or right to left.

HALF TREBLE CROCHET IN ABBREVIATIONS
Make any number of ch.
Row 1 1 htr in 3rd ch from hook, 1 htr in each of rem ch to end, turn.
Row 2 2 ch (does NOT count as a st), 1 htr in each htr to end, turn.
Rep row 2 to form htr fabric.

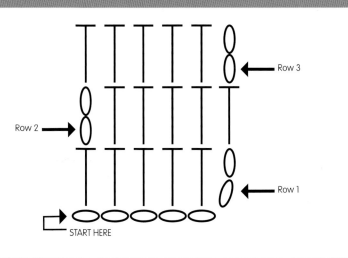

TREBLE CROCHET INSTRUCTIONS

The treble symbol has a short diagonal line across its "waist". The diagram shows clearly how the 3-chain turning chain counts as the first stitch of each row.

TREBLE CROCHET IN ABBREVIATIONS
Make any number of ch.
Row 1 1 tr in 4th ch from hook, 1 tr in each or rem ch to end, turn.
Row 2 3 ch (counts as first tr), miss first tr in row below, *1 tr in next tr; rep from * to end, then work 1 tr in top of 3-ch at end, turn.
Rep row 2 to form tr fabric.

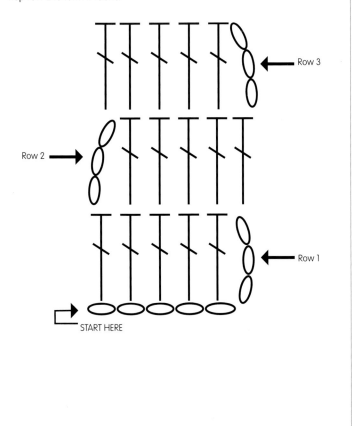

DOUBLE TREBLE CROCHET INSTRUCTIONS

Two short diagonal lines cross the "waist" of the double treble symbol, echoing the two diagonal yarn strands on the stitch itself.

DOUBLE TREBLE CROCHET IN ABBREVIATIONS
Make any number of ch.
Row 1 1 dtr in 5th ch from hook, 1 dtr in each of rem ch to end, turn.
Row 2 4 ch (counts as first dtr), miss first dtr in row below, *1 dtr in next dtr; rep from * to end, then work 1 dtr in top of 4-ch at end, turn.
Rep row 2 to form dtr fabric.

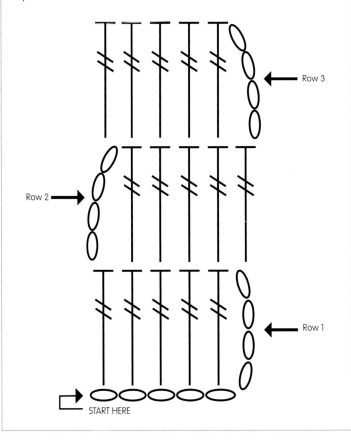

STITCH TECHNIQUES

The basic crochet stitches can be combined together in various ways to create endless textures and sculptured effects. Not all the vast range of crochet stitch techniques can be included, but the most commonly used are explained here in detail. When attempting the stitch patterns on pages 34–36, refer back to these step-by-step instructions to see more clearly how to achieve the textures.

SIMPLE TEXTURES

The simplest and most subtle crochet textures are created by working into various parts of the stitches or between the stitches in the row below. Before trying out any of these techniques, learn about the parts of the stitches so you can identify them easily.

PARTS OF STITCHES

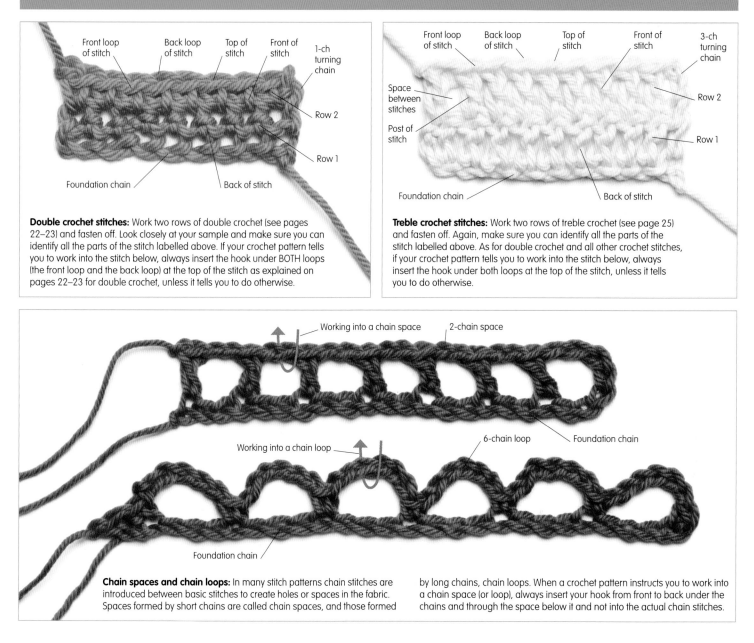

Double crochet stitches: Work two rows of double crochet (see pages 22–23) and fasten off. Look closely at your sample and make sure you can identify all the parts of the stitch labelled above. If your crochet pattern tells you to work into the stitch below, always insert the hook under BOTH loops (the front loop and the back loop) at the top of the stitch as explained on pages 22–23 for double crochet, unless it tells you to do otherwise.

Treble crochet stitches: Work two rows of treble crochet (see page 25) and fasten off. Again, make sure you can identify all the parts of the stitch labelled above. As for double crochet and all other crochet stitches, if your crochet pattern tells you to work into the stitch below, always insert the hook under both loops at the top of the stitch, unless it tells you to do otherwise.

Chain spaces and chain loops: In many stitch patterns chain stitches are introduced between basic stitches to create holes or spaces in the fabric. Spaces formed by short chains are called chain spaces, and those formed by long chains, chain loops. When a crochet pattern instructs you to work into a chain space (or loop), always insert your hook from front to back under the chains and through the space below it and not into the actual chain stitches.

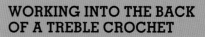

WORKING INTO THE BACK OF A DOUBLE CROCHET

Working into only the back loops of the stitches in every row of double crochet creates a deep ridged effect. The ridges are formed by the unworked loops.

WORKING INTO THE FRONT OF A DOUBLE CROCHET

Working into only the front loop of each double crochet in the row below, on every row, creates a less pronounced texture than working into only the back loop.

WORKING INTO THE BACK OF A TREBLE CROCHET

The same techniques shown for working into the back or front of a double crochet can be used on all crochet stitches to create ridges. The fabric looks the same on both sides.

WORKING INTO SPACES BETWEEN STITCHES

Another way to achieve a subtly different texture with basic stitches is to work the stitches into the spaces between the stitches in the row below, instead of into the tops of the stitches.

WORKING INTO A CHAIN SPACE

Tweed stitch illustrates the simplest of all textures created by working into a chain space. Here double crochet stitches are worked in the 1-chain spaces between the stitches in the row below instead of into the tops of the stitches.

Tweed stitch pattern
Because it is such a popular stitch and a perfect alternative for basic double crochet, the pattern for it is given here. (See page 33 for abbreviations.) Start with an even number of chains.
Row 1 1 dc in 2nd ch from hook, *1 ch, miss next ch, 1 dc in next ch; rep from * to end, turn.
Row 2 1 ch (does NOT count as a stitch), 1 dc in first dc, 1 dc in next 1-ch sp, *1 ch, 1 dc in next 1-ch sp; rep from * to last dc, 1 dc in last dc, turn.
Row 3 1 ch (does NOT count as a stitch), 1 dc in first dc, *1 ch, 1 dc in next 1-ch sp; rep from * to last 2 dc, 1 ch, miss next dc, 1 dc in last dc, turn.
Rep rows 2 and 3 to form patt.

FOLLOWING SIMPLE STITCH PATTERNS

Working a project from a crochet pattern for the first time can seem difficult for a beginner, especially if an experienced crocheter is not at hand as a guide. The best way to prepare for a crochet pattern is first to practise crocheting rectangles of various stitch patterns using simple stitch techniques. This is a good introduction to following abbreviated written row instructions and symbol diagrams.

UNDERSTANDING WRITTEN INSTRUCTIONS

As long as you are confident that you know how to work all the basic stitches as described on pages 18–29, there is nothing stopping you progressing on to the simple textured stitch patterns on pages 34–36. Simply consult the list on the opposite page for the meanings of the various abbreviations and follow the written row instructions one step at a time.

Begin by making the required number of chains for the foundation chain, using your chosen yarn and one of the hook sizes recommended for this yarn weight on page 13. Crochet a swatch that repeats the pattern only a few times to test it out. (If you decide to make a blanket or cushion cover with the stitch

later, you can adjust the hook size before starting it to obtain the exact flexibility of fabric you desire.)

Work each row of the stitch pattern slowly and mark the right side of the fabric (if there is one) as soon as you start, by tying a contrasting coloured thread to it. Another good tip is to tick off the rows as you complete them or put a sticky note under them so you don't lose your place in the pattern. If you do get lost in all the stitches, pull out all the rows and start from the foundation-chain again.

UNDERSTANDING STITCH SYMBOL DIAGRAMS

Crochet stitch patterns can also be given in symbols (see opposite page). These diagrams are usually even easier to follow than directions with abbreviations because they create a visual reference of approximately how the finished stitch will look. Each basic stitch on the chart is represented by a symbol that resembles it in some way. The position of the base of each stitch symbol indicates which stitch or chain space it is worked into in the row below. If the symbols are joined at the base, this means that they are worked into the same stitch in the row below.

The beginning of the foundation chain will be marked as your starting point on the diagram. Read each row on the diagram either from right to left or left to right following the direction of the arrow. Although you can consult the

written instructions for how many chains to make for a foundation chain and how to repeat the stitch repeat across a row (or a row repeat up the fabric), it is easy to work these out yourself from the diagram once you become proficient in reading diagrams. But to begin with, work from the written instructions and use the diagram as a visual aid. Once you have completed the first few rows of the pattern, you can dispense with the written instructions all together and continue with the diagram as your sole guide. If the stitch is an easy one, you will very quickly be able to work it without looking at any instructions at all.

This symbol diagram for the open shell stitch (see page 40) is a good introduction to working from a symbol diagram. Start at the bottom of the diagram and follow it row by row with the aid of the numbered tips.

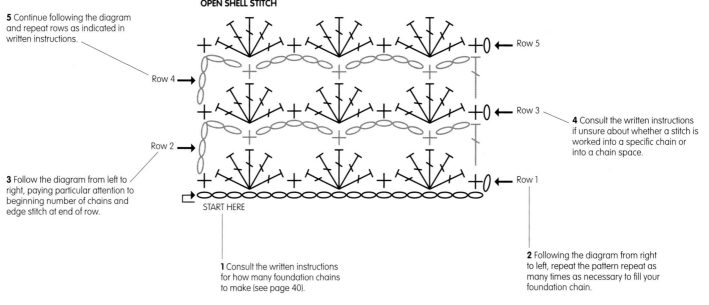

OPEN SHELL STITCH

5 Continue following the diagram and repeat rows as indicated in written instructions.

Row 4 →

Row 2 →

3 Follow the diagram from left to right, paying particular attention to beginning number of chains and edge stitch at end of row.

START HERE

← Row 5

← Row 3

4 Consult the written instructions if unsure about whether a stitch is worked into a specific chain or into a chain space.

← Row 1

1 Consult the written instructions for how many foundation chains to make (see page 40).

2 Following the diagram from right to left, repeat the pattern repeat as many times as necessary to fill your foundation chain.

CROCHET ABBREVIATIONS

These are the abbreviations most commonly used in crochet patterns. The abbreviations for the basic stitches are listed first and the other abbreviations found in crochet patterns follow. Any special abbreviations in a crochet pattern will always be explained in the pattern.

Abbreviations for basic stitches
Note: The names for the basic crochet stitches differ in the UK and the US. This book uses UK crochet terminology, so if you have learned to crochet in the US, be sure to take note of the difference in terminology.

ch	chain
ss	slip stitch
dc	double crochet (US single crochet – sc)
htr	half treble (US half double crochet – hdc)
tr	treble (US double crochet – dc)
dtr	double treble (US treble crochet – tr)
trtr	triple treble (US double treble crochet – dtr)
qtr	quadruple treble (US triple treble crochet – trtr)
quintr	quintuple treble (US quadruple treble – quadtr)

Other abbreviations
alt	alternate
beg	begin(ning)
cm	centimetre(s)
cont	continu(e)(ing)
dc2tog	see Crochet Terminology
dc3tog	see Crochet Terminology
dec	decreas(e)(ing)
foll	follow(s)(ing)
g	gram(s)
htr2tog	see Crochet Terminology
htr3tog	see Crochet Terminology
in	inch(es)
inc	increas(e)(ing)
m	metre(s)
mm	millimetre(s)
oz	ounce(s)
patt(s)	pattern(s)
rem	remain(s)(ing)
rep	repeat(s)(ing)
RS	right side
sp	space(s)
st(s)	stitch(es)
tog	together
tr2tog	see Crochet Terminology
tr3tog	see Crochet Terminology
WS	wrong side
yd	yard(s)
yrh	yarn round hook (US yarn over hook – yo)

* Repeat instructions after asterisk or between asterisks as many times as instructed.

[ ] Repeat instructions inside square brackets as many times as instructed.

CROCHET TERMINOLOGY

The following terms are commonly used in crochet patterns. Many crochet terms are the same in the UK and the US, but where they differ, the US equivalent is given in parentheses. Turn to the pages indicated for how to work the various increases, decreases, or stitch techniques listed.

bobble: Several stitches worked into the same stitch in the row below and joined together at the top.

cluster: Several stitches worked into different stitches in the row below, but joined together at the top.

dc2tog (work 2 dc together): See page 48. (US sc2tog)

dc3tog (work 3 dc together): [Insert hook in next st, yrh and draw a loop through] 3 times, yrh and draw through all 4 loops on hook – 2 sts decreased. (US sc3tog)

fasten off: Cut the yarn and draw the yarn tail through the remaining loop on the hook (see page 22).

foundation chain: The base of chain stitches that the first row of crochet is worked onto.

foundation row: The first row of a piece of crochet (the row worked onto the foundation chain) is sometimes called the foundation row.

htr2tog (work 2 htr together): [Yrh and insert hook in next st, yrh and draw a loop through] twice, yrh and draw through all 5 loops on hook – 1 st decreased. (US hdc2tog)

htr3tog (work 3 htr together): [Yrh and insert hook in next st, yrh and draw a loop through] 3 times, yrh and draw through all 7 loops on hook – 2 sts decreased. (US hdc3tog)

miss a stitch: Do not work into the stitch, but go on to the next stitch. (US "skip" a stitch).

shell: Several stitches worked into the same stitch in the previous row or into the same chain space.

pineapple: A bobble made with half trebles; also called a puff stitch.

popcorn: A type of bobble.

puff stitch: See pineapple.

tr2tog (work 2 tr together): See page 49. (US dc2tog)

tr3tog (work 3 tr together): [Yrh and insert hook in next st, yrh and draw a loop through, yrh and draw through first 2 loops on hook] 3 times, yrh and draw through all 4 loops on hook – 2 sts decreased. (US dc3tog)

turning chain: The chain/s worked at the beginning of the row (or round) to bring the hook up to the correct height for working the following stitches in the row.

CROCHET STITCH SYMBOLS

These are the symbols used in this book, but crochet symbols are not universal so always consult the key with your crochet instructions for the symbols used in your pattern.

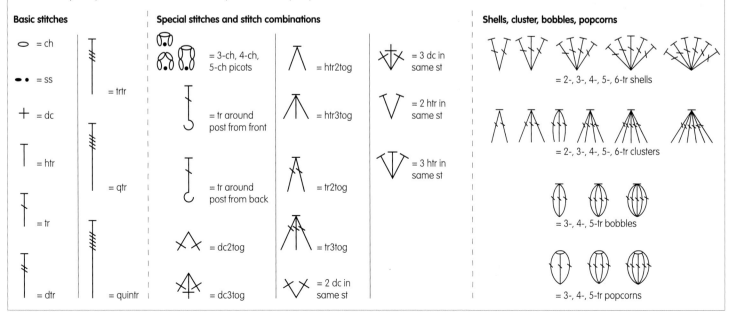

Basic stitches
- ⬭ = ch
- •• = ss
- + = dc
- T = htr
- ↑ = tr
- = dtr
- = trtr
- = qtr
- = quintr

Special stitches and stitch combinations
- = 3-ch, 4-ch, 5-ch picots
- = tr around post from front
- = tr around post from back
- = dc2tog
- = dc3tog
- = htr2tog
- = htr3tog
- = tr2tog
- = tr3tog
- = 2 dc in same st

- = 3 dc in same st
- = 2 htr in same st
- = 3 htr in same st

Shells, cluster, bobbles, popcorns
- = 2-, 3-, 4-, 5-, 6-tr shells
- = 2-, 3-, 4-, 5-, 6-tr clusters
- = 3-, 4-, 5-tr bobbles
- = 3-, 4-, 5-tr popcorns

SIMPLE TEXTURES STITCH PATTERNS

Selected for how easy they are to work, these stitch patterns cover an array of crochet textures, including those made using the techniques explained on pages 30–31. Although crochet is often identified with lacy openwork fabrics, there are also lots of solid textures like these to choose from. Quick to work and easy to memorize after the first few rows, the following stitches would make lovely cushion covers, baby blankets, or throws. They all look good on both sides of the fabrics and two are completely reversible (see Special Notes).

CROCHET RIB STITCH

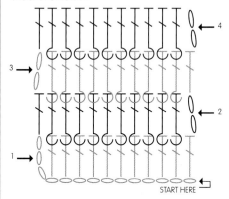

CROCHET DIAGRAM

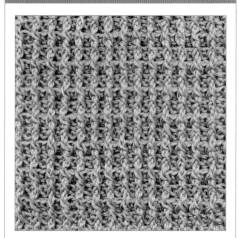

START HERE

CROCHET INSTRUCTIONS
Make a multiple of 2 ch.
Row 1 1 tr in 4th ch from hook, 1 tr in each of rem ch, turn.
Row 2 2 ch (counts as first st), miss first tr, *1 tr around post of next tr from front, 1 tr around post of next tr from back; rep from * to end, 1 tr in top of turning ch at end, turn.
Rep row 2 to form patt.

SIMPLE CROSSED STITCH

CROCHET DIAGRAM

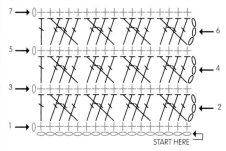

START HERE

CROCHET INSTRUCTIONS
Make a multiple of 4 ch, plus 2 extra.
Row 1 1 dc in 2nd ch from hook, 1 dc in each of rem ch, turn.
Row 2 (RS) 3 ch (counts as first tr), miss first dc, 1 tr in each of next 3 dc, yrh and insert hook from front to back in first dc (the missed dc), yrh and draw a long loop through (extending the loop that so it reaches back to position of work and does not squash 3-tr group just made), [yrh and draw through first 2 loops on hook] twice – called long tr–, *miss next dc, 1 tr in each of next 3 dc, 1 long tr in last missed dc; rep from * to last dc, 1 tr in last dc, turn.
Row 3 1 ch (does NOT count as a st), 1 dc in each tr to end (do NOT work a dc in 3-ch turning chain), turn.
Rep rows 2 and 3 to form patt.

CLOSE SHELLS STITCH

CROCHET DIAGRAM

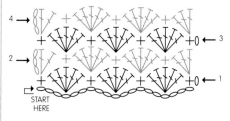

START HERE

CROCHET INSTRUCTIONS
Make a multiple of 6 ch, plus 2 extra.
Row 1 1 dc in 2nd ch from hook, *miss next 2 ch, 5 tr in next ch, miss next 2 ch, 1 dc in next ch; rep from * to end, turn.
Row 2 3 ch (counts as first tr), 2 tr in first dc, *miss next 2 tr, 1 dc in next tr, 5 tr in next dc (between shells); rep from *, ending last rep with 3 tr in last dc (instead of 5 tr), turn.
Row 3 1 ch (does NOT count as a st), 1 dc in first tr, 5 tr in next dc (between shells), miss next 2 tr, 1 dc in next tr; rep from *, working last dc in top of 3-ch at end, turn.
Rep rows 2 and 3 to form patt.

SPECIAL NOTES

• Both written and symbol instructions are given for all the Simple Textures Stitch Patterns. To get started, beginners should follow the written instructions for the first few rows, referring to the symbols for clarification. See page 33 for a list of crochet abbreviations and basic stitch symbols. If a special symbol is used in a diagram, this symbol is explained in the accompanying key. A complete explanation of how to read a crochet symbol diagram is included on page 32.

• Where there is no right side or wrong side marked in the instructions of a stitch, it looks exactly the same on both sides of the fabric. The crochet rib stitch and the close shells stitch (opposite) are examples of this – they are completely reversible.

SIMPLE BOBBLE STITCH

CROCHET DIAGRAM

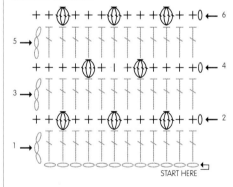

START HERE

CROCHET INSTRUCTIONS

Note: bobble = [yrh and insert hook in specified st, yrh and draw a loop through, yrh and draw through first 2 loops on hook] 4 times all in same st (5 loops now on hook), yrh and draw through all 5 loops on hook.
Make a multiple of 4 ch, plus 3 extra.
Row 1 (WS) 1 tr in 4th ch from hook, 1 tr in each of rem ch, turn.
Row 2 (RS) 1 ch (does NOT count as a st), 1 dc in each of first 2 tr, *1 bobble in next tr, 1 dc in each of next 3 tr; rep from * to last 2 tr, 1 bobble in next tr, 1 dc in next tr, 1 dc in top of 3-ch at end, turn.
Row 3 3 ch (counts as first tr), miss first dc and work 1 tr in each st to end, turn.
Row 4 1 ch (does NOT count as a st), 1 dc in each of first 4 tr, *1 bobble in next tr, 1 dc in each of next 3 tr; rep from *, ending with 1 dc in top of 3-ch at end, turn.
Row 5 Rep row 3.
Rep rows 2–5 to form patt, ending with a patt row 5.

CLUSTER AND SHELL STITCH

CROCHET DIAGRAM

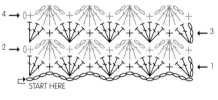

START HERE

CROCHET INSTRUCTIONS

Note: cluster (also called dc5tog) = over next 5 sts (which include 2 tr, 1 dc, 2 tr) work [yrh and insert hook in next st, yrh and draw a loop through, yrh and draw through first 2 loops on hook] 5 times (6 loops now on hook), yrh and draw through all 6 loops on hook.
Make a multiple of 6 ch, plus 4 extra.
Row 1 (RS) 2 tr in 4th ch from hook, miss next 2 ch, 1 dc in next ch, *miss next 2 ch, 5 tr in next ch, miss next 2 ch, 1 dc in next ch: rep from * to last 3 ch, miss next 2 ch, 3 tr in last ch, turn.
Row 2 1 ch (does NOT count as a st), 1 dc in first tr, *2 ch, 1 cluster over next 5 sts, 2 ch, 1 dc in next tr (centre tr of 5-tr group); rep from *, working last dc of last rep in top of 3-ch at end, turn.
Row 3 3 ch (counts as first tr), 2 tr in first dc, miss next 2 ch, 1 dc in next st (top of first cluster), *5 tr in next dc, miss next 2 ch, 1 dc in next st (top of next cluster); rep from *, ending with 3 tr in last dc, turn.
Rep rows 2 and 3 to form patt.

SHELLS AND CHAINS

CROCHET DIAGRAM

START HERE

CROCHET INSTRUCTIONS

Make a multiple of 6 ch, plus 2 extra.
Row 1 (RS) 1 dc in 2nd ch from hook, *miss next 2 ch, work [1 tr, 1 ch, 1 tr, 1 ch, 1 tr] all in next ch, miss next 2 ch, 1 dc in next ch; rep from * to end, turn.
Row 2 4 ch (counts as 1 tr and a 1-ch sp), 1 tr in first dc, miss next tr, 1 dc in next tr (centre tr of shell), *work [1 tr, 1 ch, 1 tr, 1 ch, 1 tr] all in next dc (between shells), miss next tr, 1 dc in next tr (centre tr of shell); rep from *, ending with [1 tr, 1 ch, 1 tr] in last dc, turn.
Row 3 1 ch (does NOT count as a st), 1 dc in first tr, *work [1 tr, 1 ch, 1 tr, 1 ch, 1 tr] all in next dc, miss next tr, 1 dc in next tr (centre tr of shell); rep from *, working last dc of last rep in 3rd of 4-ch made at beg of previous row, turn.
Rep rows 2 and 3 to form patt.

SPECIAL NOTES

• Refer to page 33 for a complete list of crochet abbreviations and an explanation of all the most commonly used crochet symbols. The written instructions explain how many chains to start with and which rows to repeat to form the pattern. So if working from the diagram, be sure to read the written instructions first for guidance.

• Make a test swatch of your chosen stitch pattern before starting to make a cushion cover, baby blanket, or throw from any of these textured stitches. Try out various yarns to see which suits your purpose. Tightly spun yarns are the best for showing off the sculptural aspects of textured stitches. Keep in mind that dense crochet textures need not be stiff and unyielding. If your sample swatch is not soft and pliable enough, try working another swatch with a larger hook size to loosen up the fabric a little. For baby blankets, super-fine cotton, or washable wool yarns are the most baby friendly.

POPCORN PATTERN STITCH

CROCHET DIAGRAM

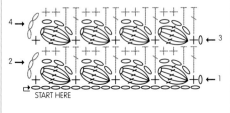

START HERE

CROCHET INSTRUCTIONS
Note: popcorn = 5 tr all in same st, carefully remove loop from hook and insert it through top of first tr of this 5-tr group, pull loop (the one removed from hook) through first tr.
Make a multiple of 4 ch, plus 2 extra.
Row 1 (RS) 1 dc in 2nd ch from hook, *3 ch, 1 popcorn in same place as last dc, miss next 3 ch, 1 dc in next ch; rep from * to end, turn.
Row 2 3 ch (counts as first tr), *work (2 dc, 1 htr) all in next 3-ch sp, 1 tr in next dc; rep from * to end, turn.
Row 3 1 ch (does NOT count as a st), 1 dc in first tr, *3 ch, 1 popcorn in same place as last dc, miss next 3 sts, 1 dc in next tr; rep from *, working last dc of last rep in top of 3-ch at end, turn.
Rep rows 2 and 3 to form patt.

SIMPLE PUFF STITCH

CROCHET DIAGRAM

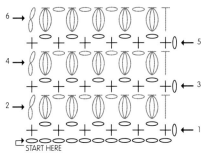

START HERE

KEY

 4-htr puff stitch

CROCHET INSTRUCTIONS
Note: puff stitch = (yrh and insert hook in st) 4 times all in same st (9 loops now on hook), yrh and draw through all 9 loops on hook to complete 4-htr puff stitch.
Make a multiple of 2 ch.
Row 1 (RS) 1 dc in 2nd ch from hook, *1 ch, miss next ch, 1 dc in next ch; rep from * to end, turn.
Row 2 2 ch (counts as first htr), 1 puff st in first 1-ch sp, *1 ch, 1 puff st in next 1-ch sp; rep from *, ending with 1 htr in last dc, turn.
Row 3 1 ch (does NOT count as a st), 1 dc in first htr, *1 ch, 1 dc in next 1-ch sp; rep from *, working last dc of last rep in top of 2-ch at end, turn.
Rep rows 2 and 3 to form patt.

SIMPLE TEXTURE STITCH

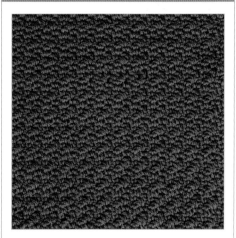

CROCHET DIAGRAM

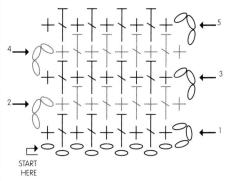

START HERE

CROCHET INSTRUCTIONS
Make a multiple of 2 ch.
Row 1 (RS) 1 dc in 4th ch from hook, *1 tr in next ch, 1 dc in next ch; rep from * to end, turn.
Row 2 3 ch (counts as first tr), miss first dc, *1 dc in next tr, 1 tr in next dc; rep from *, ending with 1 dc in top of 3-ch at end, turn.
Rep row 2 to form patt.

OPENWORK

Whether worked with fine threads for lace collars, pillow edgings, and tablecloths or with soft wools for shawls, throws, and scarves, openwork crochet has an enduring appeal. As illustrated by the easy techniques on this page and the next, these airy lace textures are produced by working chain spaces and chain loops between the basic stitches.

SIMPLE LACE TECHNIQUES

A few of the openwork stitch patterns on pages 40–42 are explained here to provide an introduction to some popular openwork crochet techniques – chain loops, shells, and picots. Refer to the instructions for the stitches when following the steps.

CHAIN LOOP MESH

1 After working the first row of chain loops into the foundation chain as explained (see page 40), work the 5-chain loops of the following rows into the loops below, joining them on with a dc as shown here.

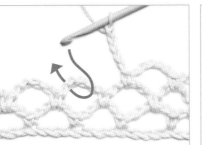

2 Remember to work the last dc of each row into the space inside the turning chain made at the beginning of the previous row. If you forget this, your lace will become narrower.

SHELL MESH STITCH

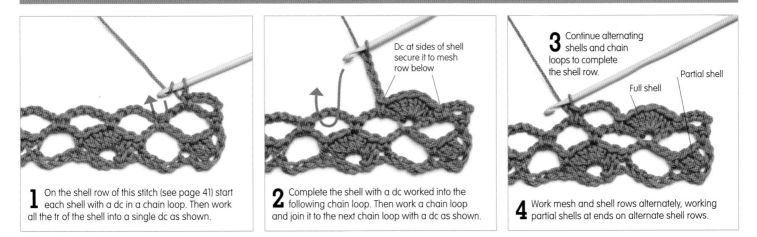

Dc at sides of shell secure it to mesh row below

3 Continue alternating shells and chain loops to complete the shell row.

Partial shell

Full shell

1 On the shell row of this stitch (see page 41) start each shell with a dc in a chain loop. Then work all the tr of the shell into a single dc as shown.

2 Complete the shell with a dc worked into the following chain loop. Then work a chain loop and join it to the next chain loop with a dc as shown.

4 Work mesh and shell rows alternately, working partial shells at ends on alternate shell rows.

PICOT NET STITCH

1 In this stitch pattern (see page 40), work 4 chains for each picot. Close the picot-ring by working a slip stitch in the fourth chain from the hook as shown.

2 Work 3 dc between each of the picots in each picot row as shown.

3 After each picot row, work a 2-chain space above each picot and a tr between the picots as shown.

FILET CROCHET

Filet crochet is the easiest of all the openwork techniques. Once you learn how to work the simple structure of the open filet mesh and the solid filet blocks, all you need to do is follow a simple chart to form the motifs and repeating patterns.

MAKING BASIC FILET MESH

When working the foundation chain for the basic filet mesh, there is no need to start with an exact number of chains, just make an extra long chain and unravel the unused excess later when finishing your crochet.

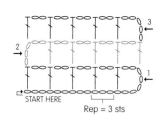

START HERE
Rep = 3 sts

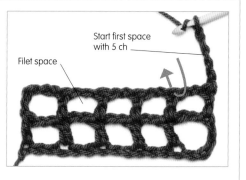

Start first space with 5 ch
Filet space

Filet mesh in symbols and words: The diagram provides the best explanation of how filet mesh is worked. If in doubt, work a mesh from the written pattern as follows:

Make a multiple of 3 ch (3 ch for each mesh square needed), plus 5 extra (to form the right side edge and top of the first mesh square of the first row).
Row 1 1 tr in 8th ch from hook, *2 ch, miss next 2 ch, 1 tr in next ch; rep from * to end.
Row 1 5 ch, miss first tr, 1 tr in next tr, *2 ch, 1 tr in next tr; rep from * working last tr in 3rd ch from last tr in row below.

MAKING FILET BLOCKS

The pattern motifs on filet crochet are created by filling in some of the mesh squares and leaving others empty. In other words, the designs are built up with solid squares and square holes. Having learned how to work the filet mesh, understanding how to fill them in to form blocks is easy.

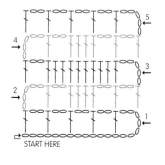

START HERE

Filet blocks in symbols: The diagram illustrates how the blocks are made – instead of working 2 chains to form an empty square, work 2 trebles fill in the square. An individual block consists of a treble on each side and 2 trebles in the centre. To work a block above a filet space, work the 2 centre trebles into the 2-chain space. To work a block above another block, work a treble into each of the trebles below.

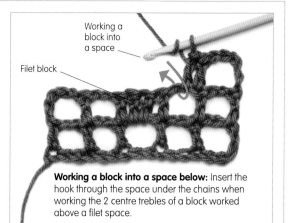

Working a block into a space
Filet block

Working a block into a space below: Insert the hook through the space under the chains when working the 2 centre trebles of a block worked above a filet space.

READING FILET CHARTS

This chart on the right shows the simple motif in the block symbol diagram above. Although actual filet charts are bigger and have elaborate patterns (see page 39), the principle is the same as for this tiny chart. Each square on the chart represents either a filet space or a filet block.

To start working from a chart, make 3 chains for each of the squares along the bottom row of the chart, plus 5 chains extra. (You can work the chart stitch-repeat as many times as desired.) Working the chart from the bottom upwards, make the blocks and spaces on the chart, while reading the first row and all following odd-numbered rows from right to left, and the even-numbered rows from left to right.

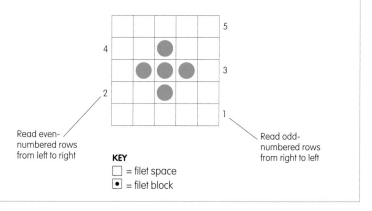

Read even-numbered rows from left to right

Read odd-numbered rows from right to left

KEY
☐ = filet space
⊡ = filet block

FILET STITCH
PATTERNS

Follow the instructions on the opposite page to work filet crochet from these charts. The best yarn to use for filet lace is a super-fine cotton yarn and a suitably small size crochet hook (see recommended hook sizes on page 13). Because filet crochet is reversible, it makes great curtains. It can also be used for edgings or insertions along the ends of pillowcases and hand towels.

SPECIAL NOTE AND SYMBOL KEY

• Repeat the charted motifs as many times as desired widthwise, and work across the stitches in rows until the chart is complete. To continue the pattern upwards, start at row 1 again.

KEY
☐ = filet space
⊡ = filet block

FLOWERS AND CIRCLES

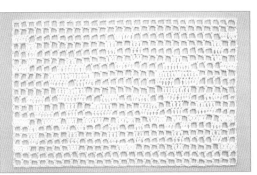

CROCHET CHART

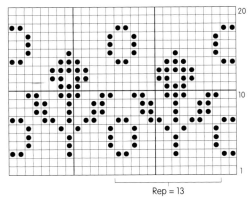

Rep = 13

DIAMONDS BORDER

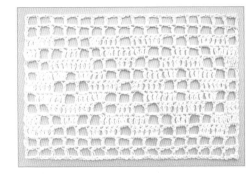

CROCHET CHART

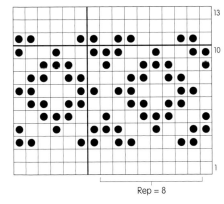

Rep = 8

ZIGZAG BORDER

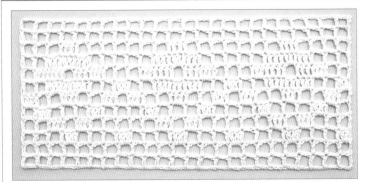

CROCHET CHART

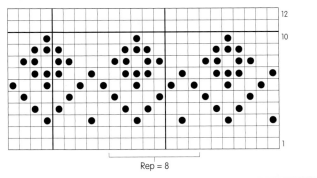

Rep = 8

SIMPLE OPENWORK STITCH PATTERNS

Openwork crochet stitches are always popular because of their lacy appearance and because they are quicker to work than solid crochet textures. They also drape gracefully due to their airy construction. Any of these easy stitch patterns would make an attractive shawl or scarf. Why not make small samples of the stitches to try them out? Then work your favourite in a range of yarns to see which texture you prefer (see Special Notes on page 42). A glance at the symbol diagram will reveal which basic stitches and simple stitch techniques are involved.

CHAIN LOOP MESH

CROCHET DIAGRAM

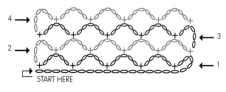

START HERE

CROCHET INSTRUCTIONS
Make a multiple of 4 ch, plus 2 extra.
Row 1 1 dc in 6th ch from hook, *5 ch, miss next 3 ch, 1 dc in next ch; rep from * to end, turn.
Row 2 *5 ch, 1 dc in next 5-ch loop; rep from * to end, turn.
Rep row 2 to form patt.

PICOT NET STITCH

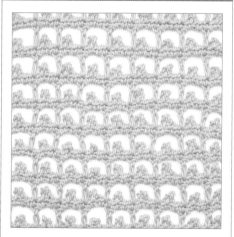

CROCHET DIAGRAM

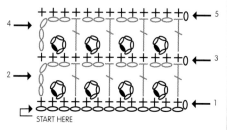

START HERE

CROCHET INSTRUCTIONS
Make a multiple of 3 ch, plus 2 extra.
Row 1 (RS) 1 dc in 2nd ch from hook, 1 dc in next ch, *4 ch, 1 ss in 4th ch from hook – called 1 picot –, 1 dc in each of next 3 ch; rep from * omitting 1 dc at end of last rep, turn.
Row 2 5 ch (counts as 1 tr and a 2-ch sp), miss first 3 dc (which includes 2 dc before picot and 1 dc after picot), 1 tr in next dc, *2 ch, miss next 2 dc (which includes 1 dc on each side of picot), 1 tr in next dc; rep from * to end, turn.
Row 3 1 ch (does NOT count as a st), 1 dc in first tr, *work [1 dc, 1 picot, 1 dc] all in next 2-ch sp, 1 dc in next tr; rep from * working last dc of last rep in 3rd ch from last tr, turn.
Rep rows 2 and 3 to form patt.

OPEN SHELL STITCH

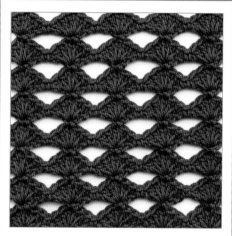

CROCHET DIAGRAM

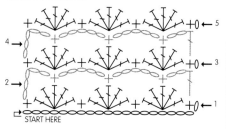

START HERE

CROCHET INSTRUCTIONS
Make a multiple of 6 ch, plus 2 extra.
Row 1 (RS) 1 dc in 2nd ch from hook, *miss next 2 ch, 5 tr in next ch, miss next 2 ch, 1 dc in next ch; rep from * to end, turn.
Row 2 5 ch (counts as first tr and a 2-ch sp), 1 dc in centre tr in of first shell, *5 ch, 1 dc in centre tr of next shell; rep from *, ending with 2 ch, 1 tr in last dc, turn.
Row 3 1 ch (does NOT count as a st), 1 dc in first tr, *5 tr in next dc, 1 dc in next 5-ch loop; rep from * working last dc of last rep in 3rd ch from last dc, turn.
Rep rows 2 and 3 to form patt.

SPECIAL NOTES

• Both written and symbol instructions are given for all the Simple Openwork Stitch Patterns. To get started, beginners should follow the written instructions for the first few rows, referring to the symbols for clarification. See page 33 for a list of crochet abbreviations and basic stitch symbols. A complete explanation of how to read a crochet symbol diagram is included on page 32.

• The written instructions explain how many chains to start with. So if working from the diagram, consult the written instructions to make the foundation chain. When working a very wide piece, such as a blanket, it is difficult to count and keep track of the number of foundation chains being made. In this case, you can make a chain a few centimetres longer than the correct approximate length and then unravel the excess later.

ARCHED MESH STITCH

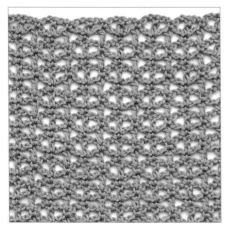

CROCHET DIAGRAM

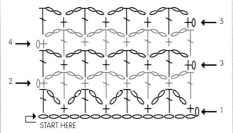

START HERE

CROCHET INSTRUCTIONS
Make a multiple of 4 ch.
Row 1 1 dc in 2nd ch from hook, 2 ch, miss next ch, 1 tr in next ch, *2 ch, miss next ch, 1 dc in next ch, 2 ch, miss next ch, 1 tr in next ch; rep from * to end, turn.
Row 2 1 ch (does NOT count as a st), 1 dc in first tr, 2 ch, 1 tr in next dc, *2 ch, 1 dc in next tr, 2 ch, 1 tr in next dc; rep from * to end, turn.
Rep row 2 to form patt.

BANDED NET STITCH

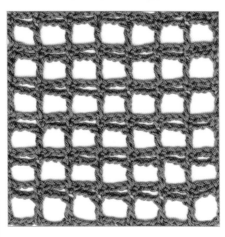

CROCHET DIAGRAM

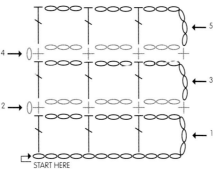

START HERE

CROCHET INSTRUCTIONS
Make a multiple of 4 ch, plus 2 extra.
Row 1 (RS) 1 tr in 10th ch from hook, 3 ch, miss next 3 ch, 1 tr in next ch; rep from * to end, turn.
Row 2 1 ch (does NOT count as a st), 1 dc in first tr, *3 ch, 1 dc in next tr; rep from *, ending with 3 ch, miss next 3 ch, 1 dc in next ch, turn.
Row 3 6 ch (counts as 1 tr and a 3-ch sp), miss first dc and first 3-ch sp, 1 tr in next dc, *3 ch, 1 tr in next dc; rep from * to end, turn.
Rep rows 2 and 3 to form patt.

SHELL MESH STITCH

CROCHET DIAGRAM

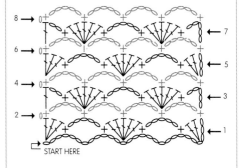

START HERE

CROCHET INSTRUCTIONS
Make a multiple of 12 ch, plus 4 extra.
Row 1 (RS) 2 tr in 4th ch from hook, *miss next 2 ch, 1 dc in next ch, 5 ch, miss next 5 ch, 1 dc in next ch, miss next 2 ch, 5 tr in next ch; rep from *, ending last rep with 3 tr (instead of 5 tr) in last ch, turn.
Row 2 1 ch (does NOT count as a st), 1 dc in first tr, *5 ch, 1 dc in next 5-ch loop, 5 ch, 1 dc in 3rd tr of next 5-tr shell; rep from * working last dc of last rep in top of 3-ch at end, turn.
Row 3 *5 ch, 1 dc in next 5-ch loop, 5 tr in next dc, 1 dc in next 5-ch loop; rep from *, ending with 2 ch, 1 tr in last dc, turn.
Row 4 1 ch (does NOT count as a st), 1 dc in first tr, *5 ch, 1 dc in 3rd tr of next 5-tr shell, 5 ch, 1 dc in next 5-ch loop; rep from * to end, turn.
Row 5 3 ch (counts as first tr), 2 tr in first dc, *1 dc in next 5-ch loop, 5 ch, 1 dc in next 5-ch loop, 5 tr in next dc; rep from * ending last rep with 3 tr (instead of 5 tr) in last dc, turn.
Rep rows 2–5 to form patt.

SPECIAL NOTES

• Lacy shawls and scarves look best worked in super-fine to lightweight yarns of various textures. Always make a swatch with your chosen yarn before beginning to make a project with one of these openwork stitch patterns. Gossamer mohair-mix yarns will work with the very simplest stitches, but to show off intricate laces, use a smooth, tightly twisted wool or cotton yarn.

• Notice how the symbol diagrams for a stitch pattern usually show more rows than appear in the accompanying written instructions. This is done on purpose so that the build-up of the rows is completely clear to the crocheter. With simple openwork patterns like these, once you have completed all the rows of the diagram you will probably have committed the pattern to memory and will not have to refer to the instructions again.

BLOCKS LACE

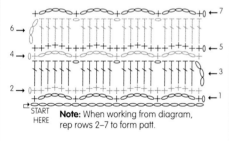

CROCHET DIAGRAM

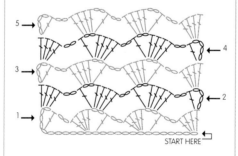

Note: When working from diagram, rep rows 2–7 to form patt.

CROCHET INSTRUCTIONS
Make a multiple of 5 ch, plus 2 extra.
Row 1 (RS) 1 dc in 2nd ch from hook, *5 ch, miss next 4 ch, 1 dc in next ch; rep from * to end, turn.
Row 2 1 ch (does NOT count as a st), 1 dc in first dc, *5 dc in next 5-ch loop, 1 dc in next dc; rep from * to end, turn.
Row 3 3 ch (counts as first tr), miss first dc, 1 tr in each of next 5 dc, *1 ch, miss next dc, 1 tr in each of next 5 dc; rep from * to last dc, 1 tr in last dc, turn.
Row 4 1 ch (does NOT count as a st), 1 dc in first tr, *5 ch, 1 dc in next 1-ch sp; rep from * working last sc of last rep in top of 3-ch at end, turn.
Rep rows 2–4 to form patt.

FANS STITCH

CROCHET DIAGRAM

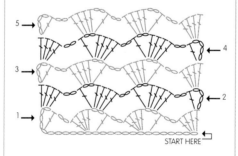

START HERE

CROCHET INSTRUCTIONS
Make a multiple of 7 ch, plus 4 extra.
Row 1 1 tr in 5th ch from hook, 2 ch, miss next 5 ch, 4 tr in next ch, *2 ch, 1 tr in next ch, 2 ch, miss next 5 ch, 4 tr in next ch; rep from * to end, turn.
Row 2 4 ch, 1 tr in first tr, *2 ch, miss next 2-ch sp and work [4 tr, 2 ch, 1 tr] all in following 2-ch sp; rep from * to last 2-ch sp, miss last 2-ch sp and work 4 tr in 4-ch loop at end, turn.
Rep row 2 to form patt.

TIARA LACE

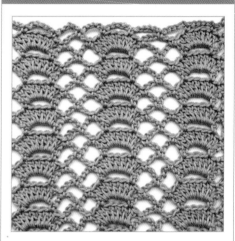

CROCHET DIAGRAM

START HERE

CROCHET INSTRUCTIONS
Make a multiple of 12 ch.
Row 1 (WS) 1 dc in 2nd ch from hook, *5 ch, miss next 3 ch, 1 dc in next ch; rep from *to last 2 ch, 2 ch, miss next ch, 1 tr in last ch, turn.
Row 2 (RS) 1 ch (does NOT count as a st), 1 dc in first st, miss next 2-ch sp, 7 tr in next 5-ch loop, 1 dc in next 5-ch loop, *5 ch, 1 dc in next 5-ch loop, 7 tr in next 5-ch loop, 1 dc in next 5-ch loop; rep from *, ending with 2 ch, 1 dtr in last dc, turn.
Row 3 1 ch (does NOT count as a st), 1 dc in first dtr, 5 ch, 1 dc in 2nd of next 7-tr shell, 5 ch, 1 dc in 6th tr of same shell, *5 ch, 1 dc in next 5-ch loop, 5 ch, 1 dc in 2nd of next 7-tr shell, 5 ch, 1 dc in 6th tr of same shell; rep from *, ending with 2 ch, 1 dtr in last dc, turn.
Rep rows 2 and 3 to form patt.

COLOURWORK

One-colour crochet has its charms, but using your creative imagination to combine colours is both more challenging and more rewarding. All of the crochet colourwork techniques are easy to master and worth experimenting with. Start by crocheting simple stripes, see below, before moving onto more decorative flower patterns (see page 53).

SIMPLE STRIPES

Stripes worked in basic stitches have more potential for creativity than most crocheters realize. The only techniques you need to learn is how and when to change colours to start a new stripe, and how to carry the yarns up the side edge of the crochet.

CHANGING COLOURS

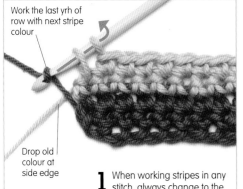

Work the last yrh of row with next stripe colour

Drop old colour at side edge

1 When working stripes in any stitch, always change to the next colour on the last yrh of the last row before the next stripe colour is started.

New colour will form first chain of next row

2 Drawing through the last yrh of the row completes the last stitch. The new colour is now on the hook ready to start the next stripe on the next row; this is so that the first turning chain in the next stripe is in the correct colour.

CARRYING COLOURS UP SIDE EDGE

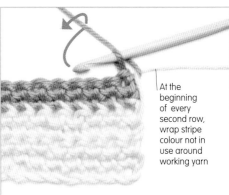

At the beginning of every second row, wrap stripe colour not in use around working yarn

If a colour is not needed for more than 2 rows, wrap it around the other colour to secure it. If it is not needed for more than 8 rows, cut it off and rejoin it later.

STRIPE COMBINATIONS

Smooth wool and fuzzy mohair stripe: The repeated double crochet stripe sequence here is two rows of a smooth wool yarn and two rows of a fuzzy mohair yarn, so each colour can simply be dropped at the side of the work and picked up when it is needed again.

Three-colour stripe: This double crochet stripe has a repeated sequence of two rows of each of three colours. Wrap the working yarn around the colours not in use on every second row to keep them snug against the edge. When changing colours, pull in the new colour firmly but not too tightly or it will pucker the edge.

Double crochet and treble crochet stripe: Each of the two stripes in this design is 2 rows tall. One stripe is worked in double crochet and the other in treble crochet. Adding in the taller trebles gives the crochet fabric a softer texture.

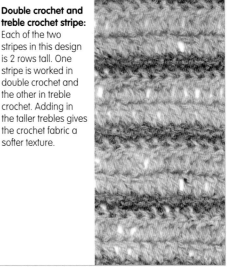

FOLLOWING A CROCHET PATTERN

Followed step by step and slowly, crochet patterns are not as difficult to work from as they appear. The guides here for a simple accessory and a garment give many tips for how to approach your first crochet patterns. This section also includes other techniques needed for working from a crochet pattern – simple increases and decreases for shaping garments, finishings such as edgings and button loops, and blocking and seams.

SIMPLE ACCESSORY PATTERNS

A beginner should choose an easy accessory pattern for a first crochet project. A striped cushion cover is given here as an example. Follow the numbered tips of the guide to familiarize yourself with the parts of a simple pattern.

1 Check the size of the finished item. If it is a simple square like this cushion, you can easily adjust the size by adding or subtracting stitches and rows.

2 It is best to use the yarn specified. But if you are unable to obtain this yarn, choose a substitute yarn as explained on page 13.

7 Make a tension swatch before starting to crochet and change the hook size if necessary (see opposite page).

8 Instructions for working a piece of crocheted fabric always start with how many chains to make for the foundation chain and which yarn or hook size to use. If there is only one hook size and one yarn, these may be absent here.

9 Consult the abbreviations list with your pattern for the meanings of abbreviations (see page 33).

13 The back of a cushion cover is sometimes exactly the same as the front or it has a fabric back. In this case, the stripes are reversed on the back for a more versatile cover.

14 After all the crocheted pieces are completed, follow the Finishing (or Making Up) section of the pattern.

STRIPED CUSHION COVER

Size of finished cushion
40.5 x 40.5cm (16 x 16in)

Materials
7 x 25g/⁷⁄₈oz (110m/120yd) balls of branded Scottish Tweed 4-Ply in Thatch 00018 **(A)**
4 x 25g/⁷⁄₈oz (110m/120yd) balls of branded Scottish Tweed 4-Ply in Skye 00009 **(B)**
3.5mm (US size E-4) crochet hook
Cushion pad to fit finished cover

Tension
22 sts and 24 rows to 10cm (4in) over double crochet using 3.5mm (US size E-4) hook or size necessary to achieve correct tension. To save time, take time to check tension.

Front
Using 3.5mm (US size E-4) hook and A, make 89 ch.
Row 1 1 dc in 2nd ch from hook, 1 dc in each of rem ch, turn. 88 dc.
Row 2 1 ch (does NOT count as a st), 1 dc in each dc to end, turn.
Rep row 2 throughout to form dc fabric.
Always changing to new colour with last yrh of last dc of previous row, work in stripes as follows:
26 rows more in A, 8 rows B, [8 rows A, 8 rows B] twice, 28 rows A.
Fasten off.

Back
Work as for Front, but use B for A, and A for B.

Finishing
Darn in loose ends.
Block and press lightly on wrong side, following instructions on yarn label.
With wrong sides facing, sew three sides of back and front together. Turn right-side out, insert cushion pad, and sew remaining seam.

3 Always purchase the same total amount in metres/yards of a substitute yarn; NOT the same amount in weight.

4 If desired, select different colours to suit your décor; the colours specified are just suggestions.

5 Alter the hook size if you cannot achieve the correct tension with the specified size (see 8 left).

6 Extra items needed for your project will usually be listed under Materials or Extras.

10 Work in the specified stitch pattern, for the specified number of rows or cm/in.

11 Colours for stripes are always changed at the end of the previous row before the colour change so the first turning chain of the new stripe is in the correct colour (see page 43).

12 Fastening off completes the crochet piece.

15 See page 27 for how to darn in loose ends.

16 Make sure you look at the yarn label instructions before attempting to press any piece of crochet. The label may say that the yarn cannot be pressed or it can be pressed only with a cool iron. (See page 50 for blocking tips.)

17 See pages 50 and 51 for seaming options. Take time with seams on crochet, and when working your very first seams, get an experienced crocheter to help you.

GARMENT PATTERNS

Garment instructions usually start with the Skill Level, followed by the Sizes, Materials, and finally the instructions. Most important for achieving a successful garment – or other fitted items such as hats, mittens, gloves, and socks – is choosing the right size and making a tension swatch.

TIPS

● **Choose a skill level** that suits your crochet experience. If in doubt or if you haven't crocheted for many years, stick to an Easy or Beginner's level until you are confident you can go to the next level.

● **White is a good colour** to use for your first crocheted sweater because the stitches are so easy to see clearly. But if you do choose white yarn, be sure to wash your hands every time you start crocheting; and when you stop, put away the yarn and sweater in a bag to keep it from becoming soiled.

● **Avoid black** or other very dark yarn for a first crocheted sweater, as the stitches are very difficult to distinguish, even for an accomplished crocheter.

● **Purchase yarn balls** that have the same dye-lot number (see pages 12–13).

● **Have a set** of hook sizes at hand if you are starting to crochet sweaters. When checking tension (see below), you will need other sizes in order to alter your hook size if necessary.

● **Always make the pieces** in the order given in the instructions, whether you are crocheting a garment, accessory or toy. On a garment, the back is usually crocheted first, followed by the front (or fronts if it is a cardigan or jacket), and lastly the sleeves. Pockets that are integrated into the fronts are crocheted before the fronts and those applied as patches are worked last.

● **It is not advisable** to attempt to alter sweater patterns. They are carefully designed for the back, front/s and sleeves to fit together precisely. For example, altering an armhole length will mean the sleeve head will not fit into it in the right way. The total length of the sleeve or sweater are sometimes adjustable, however, at the points specified in the pattern – usually right before the armhole shaping on the body and before the sleeve head shaping on the sleeve. But only adjust lengths where your instructions suggest it.

CHOOSING A GARMENT SIZE

Crochet garment sizes are usually listed as specific bust/chest sizes or in generic terms as Small, Medium, Large. (Children's sweater sizes are given in ages and chest sizes.) The best advice is not to stick strictly to choosing your preferred size by these criteria. Decide instead how you want the garment to fit you – how close-fitting or loose-fitting it should be. If you are planning to crochet a sweater, find one in your wardrobe that is comfortable and flattering and has a fabric weight and shape similar to the garment you are going to crochet. Smooth out the sweater and measure the width. Find the same, or closest, width to this on the sweater diagram of your crochet pattern – this is the size for you.

Make a photocopy of your pattern and circle or highlight all the figures that apply to your size throughout the pattern, starting with the number of balls of yarn to purchase, followed by the number of chains in the foundation chain for the sweater back, the length to the armhole, and so on. The figure for the smallest size is given first and all the figures for the larger sizes follow in parentheses. Where there is only one figure given in the instructions – be it a measurement, the number of rows, or the number of stitches – this figure applies to all sizes. Before starting your crochet, always check your tension.

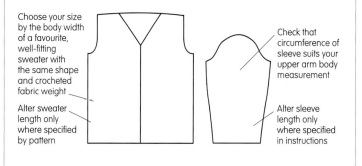

Choose your size by the body width of a favourite, well-fitting sweater with the same shape and crocheted fabric weight

Alter sweater length only where specified by pattern

Check that circumference of sleeve suits your upper arm body measurement

Alter sleeve length only where specified in instructions

MEASURING TENSION

It is essential to check your tension (stitch size) before beginning a crochet pattern. Not everyone crochets stitches with exactly the same tightness or looseness, so you may well need to use a different hook size to achieve the stitch size required by your pattern.

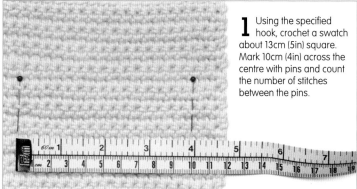

1 Using the specified hook, crochet a swatch about 13cm (5in) square. Mark 10cm (4in) across the centre with pins and count the number of stitches between the pins.

2 Count the number of rows to 10cm (4in) in the same way. If you have fewer stitches and rows than you should, try again with a larger hook size; if you have more, change to a smaller hook size. Use the hook size that best matches the correct tension. (Matching the stitch width is much more important than matching the row height.)

SHAPING CROCHET

To move from making simple squares and rectangles, a crocheter needs to know how to increase and decrease the number of stitches in the row to make shaped pieces. The most commonly used simple shaping techniques are provided here.

DOUBLE CROCHET INCREASES

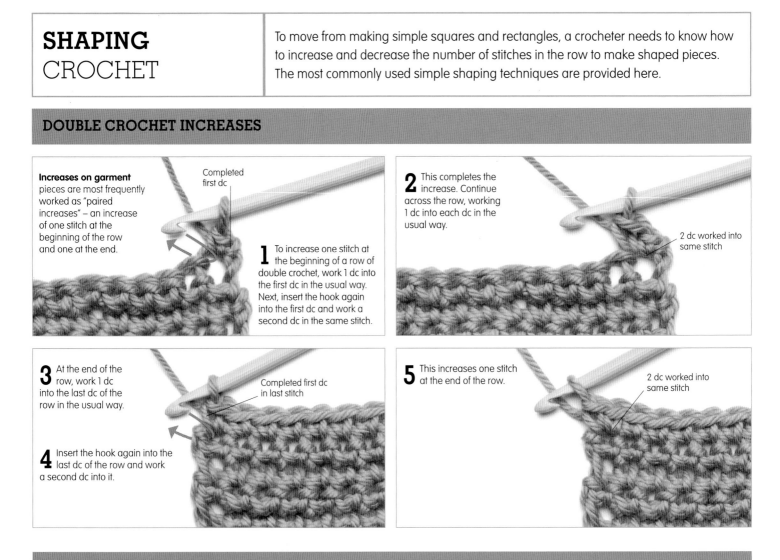

Increases on garment pieces are most frequently worked as "paired increases" – an increase of one stitch at the beginning of the row and one at the end.

Completed first dc

1 To increase one stitch at the beginning of a row of double crochet, work 1 dc into the first dc in the usual way. Next, insert the hook again into the first dc and work a second dc in the same stitch.

2 This completes the increase. Continue across the row, working 1 dc into each dc in the usual way.

2 dc worked into same stitch

3 At the end of the row, work 1 dc into the last dc of the row in the usual way.

Completed first dc in last stitch

4 Insert the hook again into the last dc of the row and work a second dc into it.

5 This increases one stitch at the end of the row.

2 dc worked into same stitch

TREBLE CROCHET INCREASES

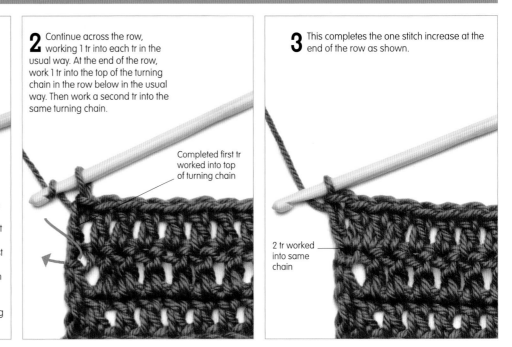

Increases on garment pieces worked in treble crochet are worked using the same techniques as for double crochet. Again, these increases are most frequently worked as "paired increases" – one stitch is increased at each end of the row.

First tr worked into first tr in row below instead of missing it

1 To increase one stitch at the beginning of a row of treble crochet, first work the turning chain, then work 1 tr into the first tr in the row below. Because the first treble in the row below is usually missed, this creates an increase at the beginning of the row.

2 Continue across the row, working 1 tr into each tr in the usual way. At the end of the row, work 1 tr into the top of the turning chain in the row below in the usual way. Then work a second tr into the same turning chain.

Completed first tr worked into top of turning chain

3 This completes the one stitch increase at the end of the row as shown.

2 tr worked into same chain

STEP INCREASE AT BEGINNING OF ROW

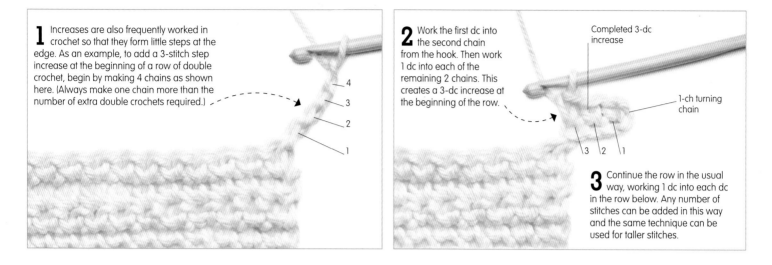

1 Increases are also frequently worked in crochet so that they form little steps at the edge. As an example, to add a 3-stitch step increase at the beginning of a row of double crochet, begin by making 4 chains as shown here. (Always make one chain more than the number of extra double crochets required.)

4
3
2
1

2 Work the first dc into the second chain from the hook. Then work 1 dc into each of the remaining 2 chains. This creates a 3-dc increase at the beginning of the row.

Completed 3-dc increase

1-ch turning chain

3 2 1

3 Continue the row in the usual way, working 1 dc into each dc in the row below. Any number of stitches can be added in this way and the same technique can be used for taller stitches.

STEP INCREASE AT END OF ROW

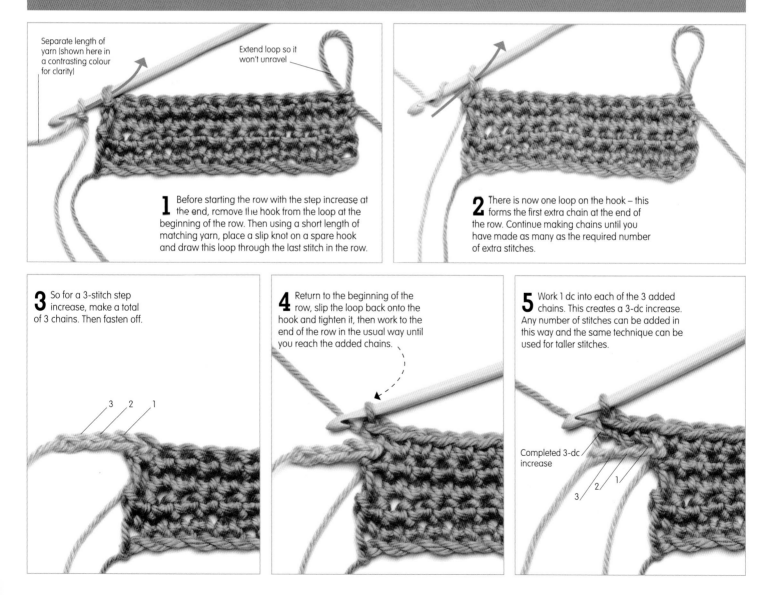

Separate length of yarn (shown here in a contrasting colour for clarity)

Extend loop so it won't unravel

1 Before starting the row with the step increase at the end, remove the hook from the loop at the beginning of the row. Then using a short length of matching yarn, place a slip knot on a spare hook and draw this loop through the last stitch in the row.

2 There is now one loop on the hook – this forms the first extra chain at the end of the row. Continue making chains until you have made as many as the required number of extra stitches.

3 So for a 3-stitch step increase, make a total of 3 chains. Then fasten off.

3 2 1

4 Return to the beginning of the row, slip the loop back onto the hook and tighten it, then work to the end of the row in the usual way until you reach the added chains.

5 Work 1 dc into each of the 3 added chains. This creates a 3-dc increase. Any number of stitches can be added in this way and the same technique can be used for taller stitches.

Completed 3-dc increase

3 2 1

DOUBLE CROCHET DECREASES (Abbreviation = dc2tog)

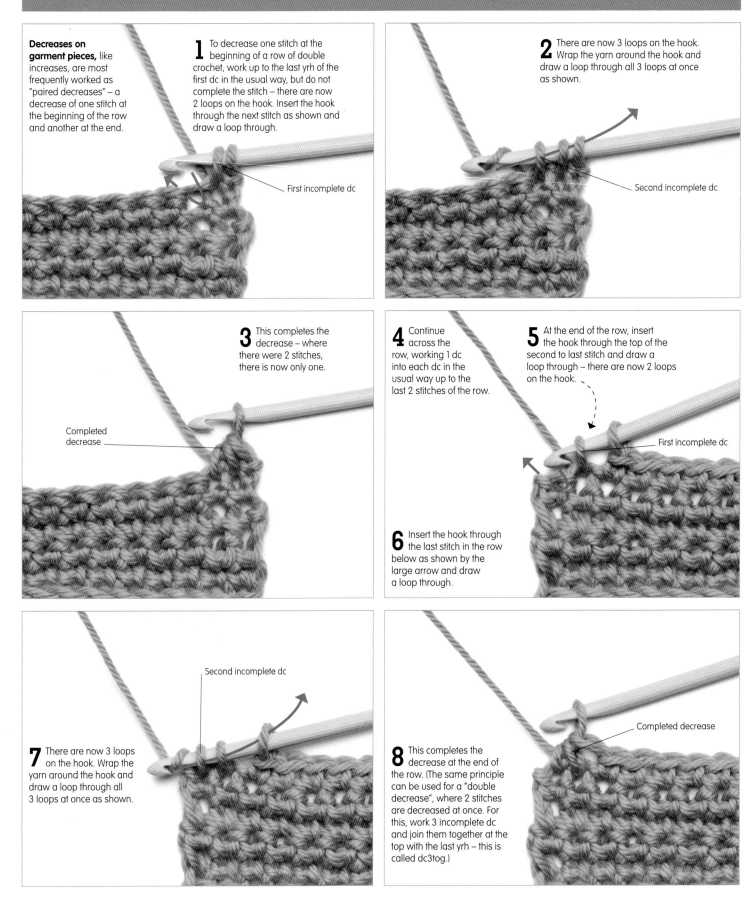

Decreases on garment pieces, like increases, are most frequently worked as "paired decreases" – a decrease of one stitch at the beginning of the row and another at the end.

1 To decrease one stitch at the beginning of a row of double crochet, work up to the last yrh of the first dc in the usual way, but do not complete the stitch – there are now 2 loops on the hook. Insert the hook through the next stitch as shown and draw a loop through.

First incomplete dc

2 There are now 3 loops on the hook. Wrap the yarn around the hook and draw a loop through all 3 loops at once as shown.

Second incomplete dc

3 This completes the decrease – where there were 2 stitches, there is now only one.

Completed decrease

4 Continue across the row, working 1 dc into each dc in the usual way up to the last 2 stitches of the row.

5 At the end of the row, insert the hook through the top of the second to last stitch and draw a loop through – there are now 2 loops on the hook.

First incomplete dc

6 Insert the hook through the last stitch in the row below as shown by the large arrow and draw a loop through.

7 There are now 3 loops on the hook. Wrap the yarn around the hook and draw a loop through all 3 loops at once as shown.

Second incomplete dc

8 This completes the decrease at the end of the row. (The same principle can be used for a "double decrease", where 2 stitches are decreased at once. For this, work 3 incomplete dc and join them together at the top with the last yrh – this is called dc3tog.)

Completed decrease

TREBLE CROCHET DECREASES (Abbreviation = *tr2tog*)

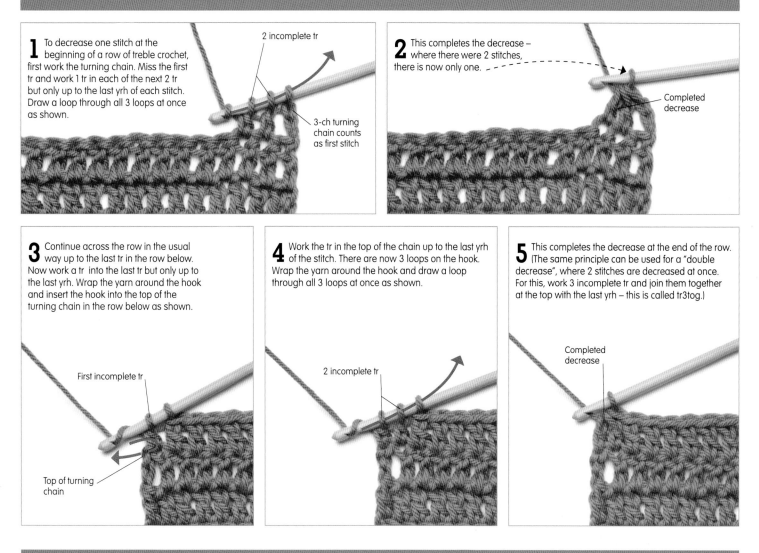

1 To decrease one stitch at the beginning of a row of treble crochet, first work the turning chain. Miss the first tr and work 1 tr in each of the next 2 tr but only up to the last yrh of each stitch. Draw a loop through all 3 loops at once as shown.

2 incomplete tr

3-ch turning chain counts as first stitch

2 This completes the decrease – where there were 2 stitches, there is now only one.

Completed decrease

3 Continue across the row in the usual way up to the last tr in the row below. Now work a tr into the last tr but only up to the last yrh. Wrap the yarn around the hook and insert the hook into the top of the turning chain in the row below as shown.

First incomplete tr

Top of turning chain

4 Work the tr in the top of the chain up to the last yrh of the stitch. There are now 3 loops on the hook. Wrap the yarn around the hook and draw a loop through all 3 loops at once as shown.

2 incomplete tr

5 This completes the decrease at the end of the row. (The same principle can be used for a "double decrease", where 2 stitches are decreased at once. For this, work 3 incomplete tr and join them together at the top with the last yrh – this is called tr3tog.)

Completed decrease

STEP DECREASES

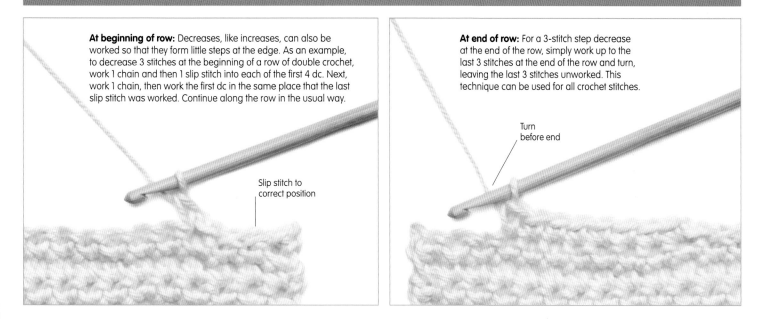

At beginning of row: Decreases, like increases, can also be worked so that they form little steps at the edge. As an example, to decrease 3 stitches at the beginning of a row of double crochet, work 1 chain and then 1 slip stitch into each of the first 4 dc. Next, work 1 chain, then work the first dc in the same place that the last slip stitch was worked. Continue along the row in the usual way.

Slip stitch to correct position

At end of row: For a 3-stitch step decrease at the end of the row, simply work up to the last 3 stitches at the end of the row and turn, leaving the last 3 stitches unworked. This technique can be used for all crochet stitches.

Turn before end

BLOCKING AND SEAMS

Always sew the seams on a garment or accessory using a blunt-ended needle and a matching yarn (a contrasting yarn is used here just to show the seam techniques more clearly); and work them in the order given in the crochet pattern. But before sewing any seams, block your crochet pieces carefully. Press the finished seams very lightly with a cool iron on the wrong side after completion.

WET BLOCKING

If your yarn will allow it, wet blocking is the best way to even out crochet. Wet the pieces in a sink full of lukewarm water. Then squeeze out the water and roll the crochet in a towel to remove excess dampness. Smooth the crochet into shape right-side down on layers of dry towels covered with a sheet, pinning at intervals. Add as many pins as is necessary to refine the shape. Do not move the crochet until it is completely dry.

STEAM BLOCKING

For a speedier process you may prefer steam blocking (if your yarn label allows it). First, pin the crochet right-side down into the correct shape. Then steam the crochet gently using a clean damp cloth, but barely touching the cloth with the iron. Never rest the weight of an iron on your crochet or it will flatten the texture. Leave the steamed piece to dry completely before unpinning it.

BACKSTITCH SEAM

Backstitch produces durable seams and is frequently recommended in crochet patterns for garments and accessories.

1 Align the crochet pieces with right sides together and secure the yarn with two or three overcast stitches in the same place. Then inserting the needle close to the edge, work the seam taking one stitch forwards and one stitch back.

Blunt-ended yarn needle

2 On the backwards stitch, be sure to insert the needle through the same place as the end of the last stitch. At the end of the seam, secure the yarn in the same way as at the beginning of the seam.

OVERCAST STITCH SEAM

Simple overcast seam: Align the crochet pieces with right sides together and secure the yarn as for backstitch. Then inserting the needle close to the edge, make stitches through the two layers as shown.

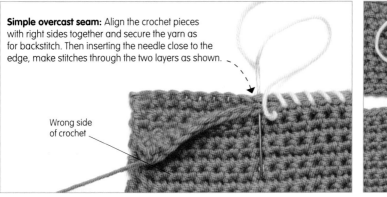

Wrong side of crochet

Right side of crochet

Pull seam yarn tight to make seam stitches disappear

Flat overcast seam: For a flat seam along the tops of stitches, lay the pieces right-side up and edge-to-edge. Work as for the simple overcast seam, but inserting the needle through only the back loops of the stitches.

EDGE-TO-EDGE SEAM

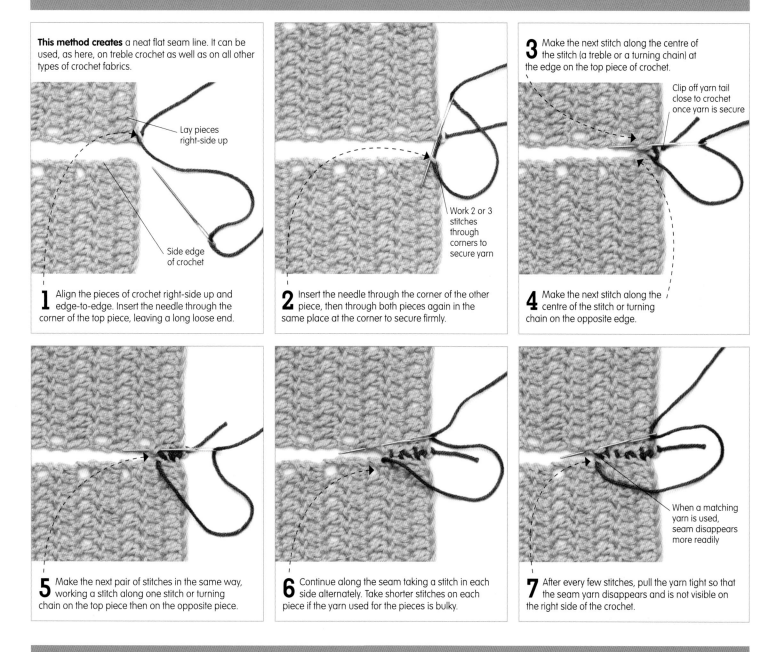

This method creates a neat flat seam line. It can be used, as here, on treble crochet as well as on all other types of crochet fabrics.

Lay pieces right-side up

Side edge of crochet

1 Align the pieces of crochet right-side up and edge-to-edge. Insert the needle through the corner of the top piece, leaving a long loose end.

Work 2 or 3 stitches through corners to secure yarn

2 Insert the needle through the corner of the other piece, then through both pieces again in the same place at the corner to secure firmly.

3 Make the next stitch along the centre of the stitch (a treble or a turning chain) at the edge on the top piece of crochet.

Clip off yarn tail close to crochet once yarn is secure

4 Make the next stitch along the centre of the stitch or turning chain on the opposite edge.

5 Make the next pair of stitches in the same way, working a stitch along one stitch or turning chain on the top piece then on the opposite piece.

6 Continue along the seam taking a stitch in each side alternately. Take shorter stitches on each piece if the yarn used for the pieces is bulky.

When a matching yarn is used, seam disappears more readily

7 After every few stitches, pull the yarn tight so that the seam yarn disappears and is not visible on the right side of the crochet.

SLIP STITCH SEAM

1 Instead of using a yarn needle to join your seam, you can use a crochet hook to work a quicker seam. Although seams can be worked with double crochet, slip stitch seams are less bulky. Start by placing a slip knot on the hook.

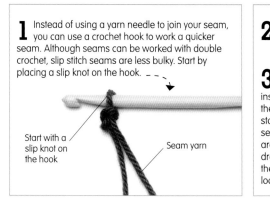

Start with a slip knot on the hook

Seam yarn

2 Align the two layers of crochet with the right sides together.

3 Then with the slip knot on the hook, insert the hook through the two layers at the starting end of the seam, wrap the yarn around the hook and draw a loop through the two layers and the loop on the hook.

4 Continue in this way and fasten off at the end. When working the seam along the tops of stitches (as here), insert the hook through only the back loops of the stitches. Along row-end edges, work through the layers one stitch in from the edge.

FINISHING
DETAILS

Finishings are often more difficult for crocheters than making the pieces. Some of the techniques most frequently used are shown here. Take your time with all finishings, and practise the methods on small swatches before adding them to your completed pieces.

DOUBLE CROCHET EDGING

Along top or bottom of a piece of crochet: Adding a simple double crochet edging is a good way to tidy up the edges of a piece of crochet. To work a double crochet edging along the top or bottom of a piece of crochet, join the yarn to the first stitch with a slip stitch, work 1 ch, 1 dc in the same place as the slip stitch, then work 1 dc in each stitch below all along the edge.

Along row-ends of a piece of crochet: A double crochet edging is worked the same way along the row-ends of a piece of crochet, but it is not as easy to achieve an even edging. To create a perfect result, experiment with how many stitches to work per row-end. If the finished edging looks flared, try working fewer stitches per row-end; and if it looks puckered, try again working more stitches per row-end.

CROCHETING EDGING DIRECTLY ONTO EDGE

Any of the edgings starting with a row of double crochet on pages 54–55 can easily be worked directly onto the crochet.

1 Using a contrasting colour for the edging, start by working the row of double crochet onto the base, then turn and work the next row of the edging (the second row of the simple shell edging on page 55 is being worked here).

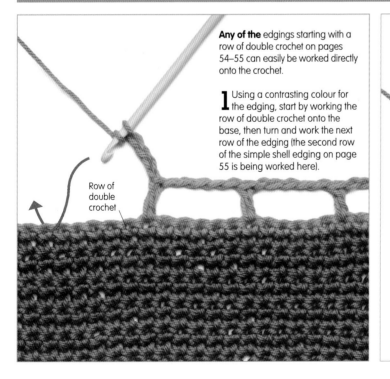

Row of double crochet

2 At the end of the second row, turn the crochet and work the remaining rows of the edging (the third and final row of the simple shell edging is being worked here).

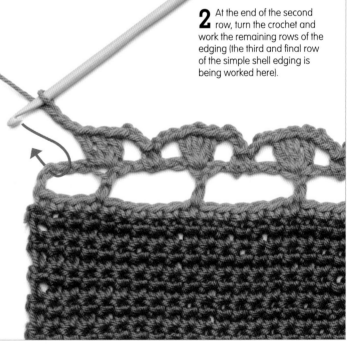

Embellishments

There are many ways to add subtle or bold embellishments to your crochet. Adornments that will dress up your stitching include beads, ribbons, flowers, fringing, and edgings.

SIMPLE FLOWER PATTERNS

Crochet flowers are very seductive – even simple ones like these, which are all easy and very quick to stitch. They make great brooches – sew a safety pin to the back and maybe a button or an artificial pearl to the flower centre.

SHORT LOOP FLOWER

CROCHET DIAGRAM

CROCHET INSTRUCTIONS
This flower is worked in 2 colours (A, B).
Using A, make 4 ch and join with a ss to first ch to form a ring.
Round 1 (RS) 1 ch (does NOT count as a st), 8 dc in ring, join with a ss to first dc of round.
Round 2 1 ch (does NOT count as a st), 2 dc in same place as ss, *2 dc in next dc; rep from * to end, join with a ss to first dc of round. 16 dc. Fasten off A.
Round 3 Using B, join with a ss to a dc, 1 ch, work [1 dc, 9 ch, 1 dc] all in same place as last ss, 1 dc in next dc; *work [1 dc, 9 ch, 1 dc] all in next dc, 1 dc in next dc; rep from * 6 times more, join with a ss to first dc of round. Fasten off.

LONG LOOP FLOWER

CROCHET DIAGRAM

Total of 17 ch in each loop

CROCHET INSTRUCTIONS
This flower is worked in 3 colours (A, B, C).
Using A, make 4 ch and join with a ss to first ch to form a ring.
Round 1 (RS) 1 ch (does NOT count as a st), 8 dc in ring, join with a ss to first dc of round. Fasten off A.
Round 2 Using B, join with a ss to a dc, 1 ch (does NOT count as a st), 2 dc in same place as last ss, *2 dc in next dc; rep from * to end, join with a ss to first dc of round. 16 dc. Fasten off B.
Round 3 Using C, join with a ss to a dc, 1 ch, work [1 dc, 17 ch, 1 dc] all in same place as last ss, *work [1 dc, 17 ch, 1 dc] all in next dc; rep from * 14 times more, join with a ss to first dc of round.
Fasten off.

BUTTON FLOWER

CROCHET DIAGRAM

CROCHET INSTRUCTIONS
Note: cluster = [yrh twice and insert hook in sp, yrh and draw a loop through, (yrh and draw through first 2 loops on hook) twice] 4 times all in same sp (5 loops now on hook), yrh and draw through all 5 loops on hook.
This flower is worked in 2 colours (A, B).
Using A, make 4 ch and join with a ss to first ch to form a ring.
Round 1 (RS) 4 ch (counts as first dtr), 20 dtr in ring, join with a ss to 4th of 4-ch. Fasten off A.
Round 2 Using B, join with a ss to same place as last ss, 1 ch (does NOT count as a st), 1 dc in same place as last ss, [5 ch, miss next 2 dtr, 1 dc in next dtr] 6 times, 5 ch, join with a ss to first dc of round.
Round 3 *Work [1 ss, 4 ch, 1 cluster, 4 ch, 1 ss] all in next 5-ch loop; rep from * 6 times more, join with a ss to last dc in round 2.
Fasten off. Sew a small button to centre of flower.

SIMPLE EDGING PATTERNS

Adding a decorative crochet edging to an otherwise mundane-looking piece of crochet (or knitting) can transform it, giving it a touch of elegance. All the simple crochet edgings that follow are worked widthwise, so you start with a length of chain roughly equivalent to the length of edging you need. Suitable even for beginners, these edgings are perfect for dressing up towel ends, throws, baby blankets, necklines, and cuffs. When making an edging that will encircle a blanket, be sure to add extra for turning the corners; the edging can then be gathered at each corner to allow for the turning. Use a short test swatch to calculate how much extra you will need at each corner. See page 33 for abbreviations and symbols.

DIAMOND EDGING

CROCHET DIAGRAM

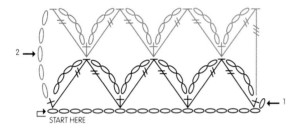

START HERE

CROCHET INSTRUCTIONS
Make a multiple of 6 ch, plus 2 extra.
Row 1 (RS) 1 dc in 2nd ch from hook, *4 ch, yrh twice and insert hook in same place as last dc, [yrh and draw first 2 loops on hook] twice, yrh twice, miss next 5 ch and insert hook in next ch, [yrh and draw first 2 loops on hook] twice, yrh and draw through all 3 loops on hook – called dtr2tog –, 4 ch, 1 dc in same place as last dtr; rep from * to end, turn.
Row 2 5 ch, 1 dtr in first dtr2tog, 4 ch, 1 dc in same place as last dtr, *4 ch, dtr2tog over last dtr worked into and next dtr, 4 ch, 1 dc in same place as last dtr; rep from *, 4 ch, yrh twice and insert hook in same place as last dc, [yrh and draw first 2 loops on hook] twice, yrh 3 times and insert hook in last dc in previous row, [yrh and draw first 2 loops on hook] 3 times, yrh and draw through all 3 loops on hook.
Fasten off.

BOLD SCALLOP EDGING

CROCHET DIAGRAM

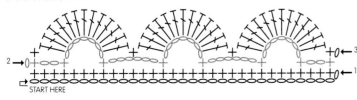

START HERE

CROCHET INSTRUCTIONS
Make a multiple of 10 ch, plus 2 extra.
Row 1 (RS) 1 dc in 2nd ch from hook, 1 dc in each of rem ch, turn.
Row 2 1 ch, 1 dc in first dc, 2 ch, miss next 2 dc, 1 dc in next dc, 7 ch, miss next 3 dc, 1 dc in next dc, *6 ch, miss next 5 dc, 1 dc in next dc, 7 ch, miss next 3 dc, 1 dc in next dc; rep from * to last 3 dc, 2 ch, miss next 2 dc, 1 dc in last dc, turn.
Row 3 1 ch, 1 dc in first dc, 14 tr in 7-ch loop, *1 dc in next 6-ch sp, 14 tr in next 7-ch loop; rep from *, ending with 1 dc in last dc.
Fasten off.

TRIPLE PICOT EDGING

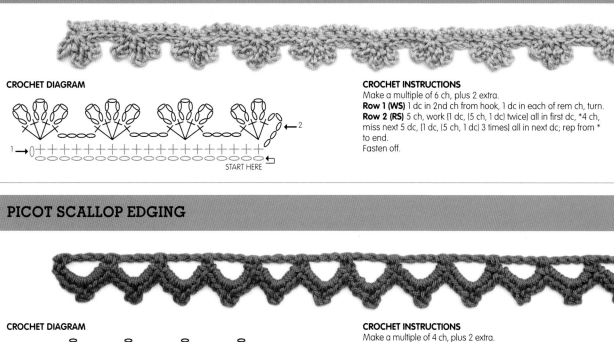

CROCHET DIAGRAM

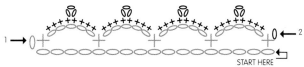

CROCHET INSTRUCTIONS
Make a multiple of 6 ch, plus 2 extra.
Row 1 (WS) 1 dc in 2nd ch from hook, 1 dc in each of rem ch, turn.
Row 2 (RS) 5 ch, work [1 dc, (5 ch, 1 dc) twice] all in first dc, *4 ch, miss next 5 dc, [1 dc, (5 ch, 1 dc) 3 times] all in next dc; rep from * to end.
Fasten off.

PICOT SCALLOP EDGING

CROCHET DIAGRAM

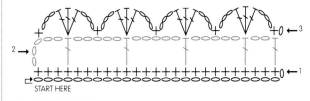

CROCHET INSTRUCTIONS
Make a multiple of 4 ch, plus 2 extra.
Row 1 (WS) 1 dc in 2nd ch from hook, *5 ch, miss next 3 ch, 1 dc in next ch; rep from * to end, turn.
Row 2 (RS) 1 ch, *work [4 dc, 3 ch, 4 dc] all in next 5-ch loop; rep from * to end.
Fasten off.

SIMPLE SHELL EDGING

CROCHET DIAGRAM

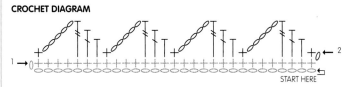

CROCHET INSTRUCTIONS
Make a multiple of 6 ch, plus 2 extra.
Row 1 (RS) 1 dc in 2nd ch from hook, 1 dc in each of rem ch, turn.
Row 2 5 ch, miss first 3 dc, 1 tr in next dc, *5 ch, miss next 5 dc, 1 tr in next dc; rep from * to last 3 dc, 2 ch, miss next 2 dc, 1 tr in last dc, turn.
Row 3 1 ch, 1 dc in first tr, 3 ch, 3 tr in next tr, *3 ch, 1 dc in next 5-ch space, 3 ch, 3 tr in next tr; rep from *, ending with 3 ch, miss first 2 ch of last 5-ch, 1 dc in next ch.
Fasten off.

GRAND EYELET EDGING

CROCHET DIAGRAM

CROCHET INSTRUCTIONS
Make a multiple of 7 ch, plus 2 extra.
Row 1 (WS) 1 dc in 2nd ch from hook, 1 dc in each of rem ch, turn.
Row 2 (RS) 1 ch, 1 dc in first dc, 1 htr in next dc, 1 tr in next dc, 1 dtr in next dc, *5 ch, miss next 3 dc, 1 dc in next dc, 1 htr in next dc, 1 tr in next dc, 1 dtr in next dc; rep from * to last 4 dc, 5 ch, miss next 3 dc, 1 dc in last dc.
Fasten off.

CIRCULAR CROCHET

Crochet can be worked not only back and forth in rows, but round and round in circles to form tubes or flat shapes started from the centre (called medallions). The basic techniques for crocheting in the round are very easy to learn, even for a beginner, so it is not surprising that many popular crochet accessories are made with circular crochet, including flowers and afghan motifs, as well as seamless toys, hats, mittens, containers, and bags.

CROCHETING TUBES

Tubular crochet is started on a long foundation chain joined into a ring, and the rounds of stitches are worked around this ring. The easiest of all crochet cylinders is double crochet worked in a spiral without turning chains.

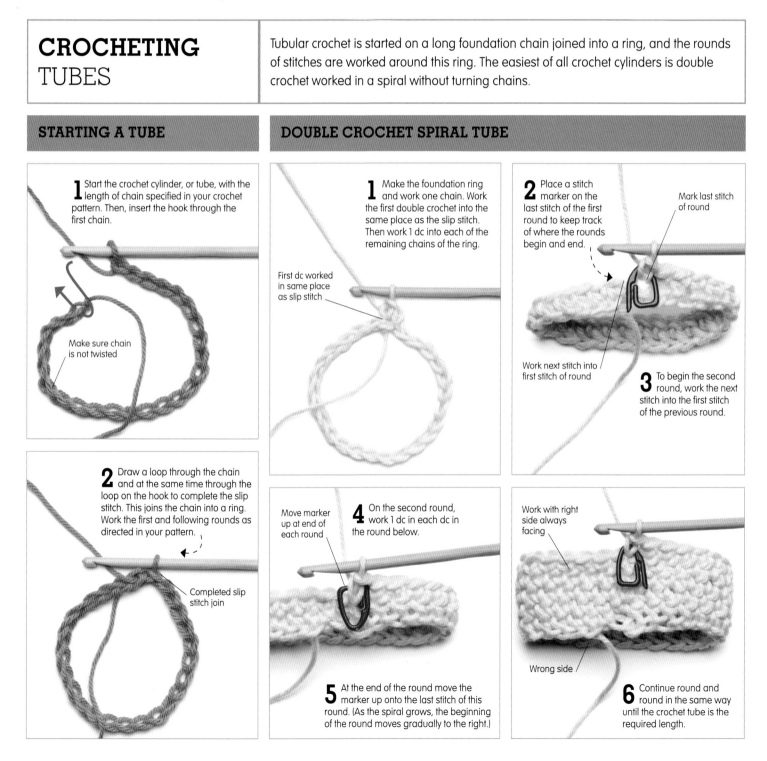

STARTING A TUBE

1 Start the crochet cylinder, or tube, with the length of chain specified in your crochet pattern. Then, insert the hook through the first chain.

Make sure chain is not twisted

2 Draw a loop through the chain and at the same time through the loop on the hook to complete the slip stitch. This joins the chain into a ring. Work the first and following rounds as directed in your pattern.

Completed slip stitch join

DOUBLE CROCHET SPIRAL TUBE

1 Make the foundation ring and work one chain. Work the first double crochet into the same place as the slip stitch. Then work 1 dc into each of the remaining chains of the ring.

First dc worked in same place as slip stitch

2 Place a stitch marker on the last stitch of the first round to keep track of where the rounds begin and end.

Mark last stitch of round

Work next stitch into first stitch of round

3 To begin the second round, work the next stitch into the first stitch of the previous round.

4 On the second round, work 1 dc in each dc in the round below.

Move marker up at end of each round

5 At the end of the round move the marker up onto the last stitch of this round. (As the spiral grows, the beginning of the round moves gradually to the right.)

Work with right side always facing

Wrong side

6 Continue round and round in the same way until the crochet tube is the required length.

FLAT
CIRCLES

The circular crochet techniques for making flat shapes are a little more difficult than those for making tubes. Making a simple circle is a good example for how other flat medallion shapes are started and then worked round and round from the centre. The circle is also used in conjunction with the crochet tube to make containers or the parts of toys, so it is well worth practising.

CROCHETING A CIRCLE

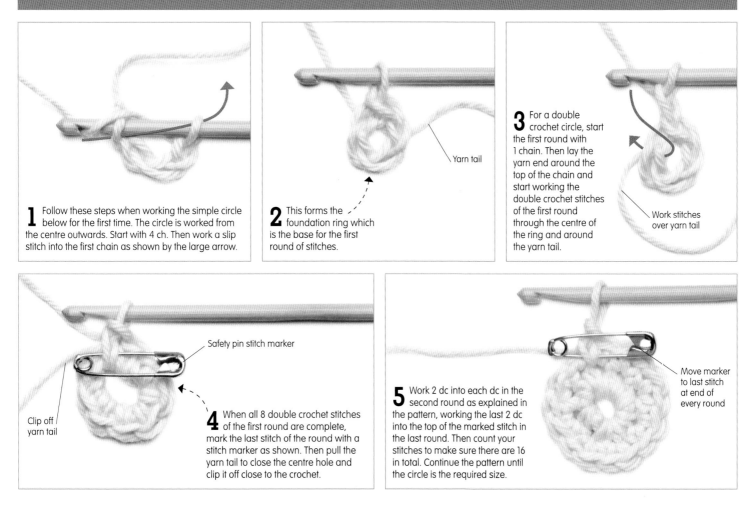

1 Follow these steps when working the simple circle below for the first time. The circle is worked from the centre outwards. Start with 4 ch. Then work a slip stitch into the first chain as shown by the large arrow.

2 This forms the foundation ring which is the base for the first round of stitches.

Yarn tail

3 For a double crochet circle, start the first round with 1 chain. Then lay the yarn end around the top of the chain and start working the double crochet stitches of the first round through the centre of the ring and around the yarn tail.

Work stitches over yarn tail

Safety pin stitch marker

Clip off yarn tail

4 When all 8 double crochet stitches of the first round are complete, mark the last stitch of the round with a stitch marker as shown. Then pull the yarn tail to close the centre hole and clip it off close to the crochet.

5 Work 2 dc into each dc in the second round as explained in the pattern, working the last 2 dc into the top of the marked stitch in the last round. Then count your stitches to make sure there are 16 in total. Continue the pattern until the circle is the required size.

Move marker to last stitch at end of every round

SIMPLE 11-ROUND CIRCLE MEDALLION

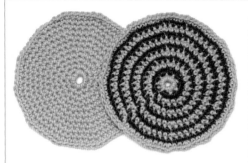

This pattern is for a classic simple crochet circle. (See page 33 for abbreviations.)

Note: Work the circle in a single colour or in two colours (A and B). For a two-colour circle, work the foundation ring and round 1 in A, then work the following rounds in B and A alternately, changing to the new colour with the last yrh of the last dc of each round and carrying the colours up the wrong side of the circle.
Make 4 ch and join with a ss in first ch to form a ring.
Round 1 (RS) 1ch, 8 dc in ring. Do not turn at end of rounds, but work with RS always facing.

Note: Mark the last stitch of round 1, and at the end of each of the following rounds, move this marker to the last stitch of the round just worked.
Round 2 2 dc in each dc. *16 dc.*
Round 3 *1 dc in next dc, 2 dc in next dc; rep from *. *24 dc.*
Round 4 1 dc in each dc.
Round 5 *1 dc in next dc, 2 dc in next dc; rep from *. *36 dc.*
Round 6 Rep round 4.
Round 7 *1 dc in each of next 2 dc, 2 dc in next dc; rep from *. *48 dc.*
Round 8 Rep round 4.

Round 9 *1 dc in each of next 3 dc, 2 dc in next dc; rep from *. *60 dc.*
Round 10 Rep round 4.
Round 11 1 dc in each of first 2 dc, 2 dc in next dc, *1 dc in each of next 4 dc, 2 dc in next dc; rep from *, ending with 1 dc in each of last 2 dc. *72 dc.*
Work 1 ss in next dc and fasten off.
To make a bigger circle, continue in this way, adding 12 extra dc in every alternate round (by working one more stitch between increases) and altering the position of the first increase on every increase round.

CLOTHES AND ACCESSORIES

PROJECT BASKET

This handy, versatile basket is made in the round, starting at the centre bottom. The bottom edge and brim fold are cleverly made by crocheting only into the back loop of the stitch for one round. Size can be adjusted by adding or subtracting increase and even rounds.

MATERIALS

Size
13cm x 16cm (5in x 6in)

Yarn
Stylecraft Special DK/Takhi Cotton Classic 100g

A × 1   **B** × 1 ball

Crochet hook
4mm (G-6 US) hook

PATTERN

BASKET
With yarn A, work 2 ch, 6 dc in 2nd ch from hook.
Round 1 2 dc in each dc to end. (12sts)
Round 2 *1 dc in next dc, 2 dc in next dc; rep from * to end. (18sts)
Round 3 *1 dc in each of next 2 dc, 2 dc in next dc; rep from * to end. (24sts)
Round 4 *1 dc in each of next 3 dc, 2 dc in next dc; rep from * to end. (30sts)
Round 5 *1 dc in each of next 4 dc, 2 dc in next dc; rep from * to end. (36sts)
Round 6 *1 dc in each of next 5 dc, 2 dc in next dc; rep from * to end. (42sts)
Round 7 *1 dc in each of next 6 dc, 2 dc in next dc; rep from * to end. (48sts)
Round 8 *1 dc in each of next 7 dc, 2 dc in next dc; rep from * to end. (54sts)
Round 9 *1 dc in each of next 8 dc, 2 dc in next dc; rep from * to end. (60sts)
Round 10 *1 dc in each of next 9 dc, 2 dc in next dc; rep from * to end. (66sts)
Round 11 *1 dc in each of next 10 dc, 2 dc in next dc; rep from * to end. (72sts)
Round 12 *1 dc in each of next 11 dc, 2 dc in next dc; rep from * to end. (78sts)
Round 13 *1 dc in each of next 12 dc, 2 dc in next dc; rep from * to end. (84sts)

Round 14 *1 dc in each of next 13 dc, 2 dc in next dc; rep from * to end. (90sts)
Round 15 *1 dc in each of next 14 dc, 2 dc in next dc; rep from * to end. (96sts)
Round 16 *1 dc in each of next 15 dc, 2 dc in next dc; rep from * to end. (102sts)
Increase can be stopped earlier for a smaller basket or continued as set for a larger basket
Round 17 Working into back loops only, dc in each dc to end. (102sts)
Continue working even rounds through both loops (1 dc in each dc to end) until piece measures 13cm (5in) from Round 17, or desired height.

FOLDOVER
Round 1 Working in the front loops only, with yarn B, 1 dc in each dc to end. (102sts)
Round 2 With yarn A, 1 dc in each dc through both loops to end. (102sts)
Round 3 With yarn B, 1 dc in each dc through both loops to end. (102sts)
Rep last 2 rounds once more.
Fasten off, weave in ends.

The decorative brim with three contrasting stripes is crocheted as part of the basket and then folded down.

As rounds increase on the bottom of the basket, it begins to look more and more like a hexagon.

LACY SCARF

This lacy, openwork scarf is made using the fans stitch (see page 42) from the Techniques section. The openwork pattern is created using alternating chain loops and treble crochet stitches. It is an easy first project as it's very forgiving!

MATERIALS

Size
18cm x 180cm (7in x 71in) or desired length

Yarn
Sirdar Country Style DK/Berroco Vintage DK 100g

x 1 ball

Crochet hook
4mm (G-6 US) hook

PATTERN

Work 33 ch
Row 1 1 tr in 5th ch from hook, *2 ch, miss 5 chs, 3 tr in next ch, 2 ch, tr in next ch; rep from * 3 times more.
Row 2 4 ch, turn. 1 tr in first 2-ch sp, *2 ch, work (4 tr, 2 ch, 1 tr) in next 2-ch sp; rep from * twice more, 2 ch, work 3 tr in last sp and 1 tr in 3rd of 4 chs of turning ch from row below.
Rep row 2 until piece is 180cm (71in) or desired length.
Fasten off, weave in ends.

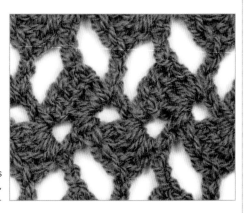

The alternating pattern forms rows of asymmetrical stitches and spaces, giving the scarf a light, lacy appearance.

There is no need to add edging to either the long sides or the ends of this scarf as the stitch pattern forms its own.

SHAWL

This lacy, feminine shawl uses a variation of the chain loop mesh (see page 37) from the Techniques section, as well as the picot and shell edgings (see page 55). The shawl is made in rows, starting from the top and decreasing naturally down to a point at the bottom.

MATERIALS

Size
135cm x 105cm (53in x 41in)

Yarn
Sublime Cashmerino Silk DK 50g

x 5 balls

Crochet hook
4.5mm (7 US) hook

PATTERN

Work 181 ch (or any multiple of 3+1).
Row 1 Miss first ch, dc in each ch to end, turn. (180sts)
Row 2 *6 ch, miss 2 sts, dc in next st; rep from * to end, turn.
Row 3 and all following rows Ss in first 3 chs, *6 ch, dc in next 6-ch loop; rep from * to end, turn.
Rep last row until left with one 6-ch loop.
Fasten off, weave in ends.

TOP PICOT EDGING
Working along top of shawl, attach yarn at one end, 1 ch, dc in same st, *4 ch, ss in 4th ch from hook, dc in each of next 2 sts; rep from * across top edge, ending (4 ch, ss in 4th ch from hook, dc) all in last st. Leave yarn attached.

SIDE SHELL EDGING
Working around two remaining sides, *ss in next 6-ch loop, 5 tr in same sp, ss in same sp; rep from * around two un-edged sides, working (ss, 10 tr, ss) in loop at bottom point.
Fasten off, weave in ends.

Picot edging is used to finish the top of the shawl. The edging can be made larger by adding chains.

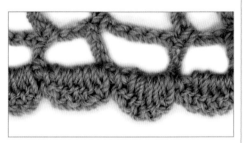

Shell edging finishes the long sides of the shawl. Each shell in the edging matches up with a single space in the lace pattern.

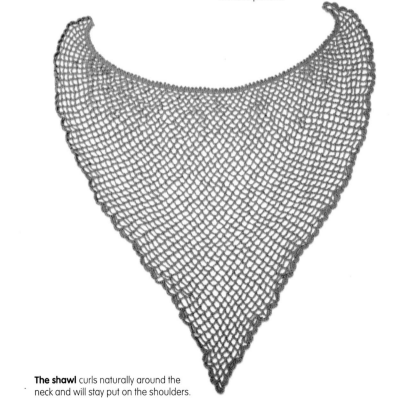

The shawl curls naturally around the neck and will stay put on the shoulders.

BEANIE HAT

This cosy hat is made in the round starting at the top and increasing to the circumference of the head to fit the recipient. This hat has been made with two contrasting stripes near the brim, but it could easily be customized with additional stripes and colours.

MATERIALS

Size
To fit an adult male

Yarn
A Wendy Aran/Wool-Ease® Worsted 400g
B Debbie Bliss Cashmerino Aran 50g

A × 1   B × 1 ball

Crochet hook
5mm (H-8 US) hook

Tension
11sts per 10cm (4in)

Special abbreviations
fphtr: front post half treble. Yrh and insert hook from front to back to front around the post of next st. Yrh and pull up a loop. Yrh and pull through all three loops on hook.

PATTERN

With yarn A, work 4 ch, ss in first ch to form loop.
Round 1 2 ch, 11 htr in loop, ss in top of first 2-ch to join. (12sts)
Round 2 2 ch, 2 htr in next st. *1 htr in next st, 2 htr in next st; rep from * to end, ss in top of first 2-ch to join. (18sts)
Round 3 2 ch, 1 htr in next st, 2 htr in next st. *1 htr in each of next 2 sts, 2 htr in next st; rep from * to end, ss in top of first 2-ch to join. (24sts)
Round 4 2 ch, 1 htr in each of next 2 sts, 2 htr in next st. *1 htr in each of next 3 sts, 2 htr in next st; rep from * to end, ss in top of first 2-ch to join. (30sts)
Round 5 2 ch, 1 htr in each of next 3 sts, 2 htr in next st. *1 htr in each of next 4 sts, 2 htr in next st; rep from * to end, ss in top of first 2-ch to join. (36sts)
Round 6 2 ch, 1 htr in each of next 4 sts, 2 htr in next st. *1 htr in each of next 5 sts, 2 htr in next st; rep from * to end, ss in top of first 2-ch to join. (42sts)
Round 7 2 ch, 1 htr in each of next 5 sts, 2 htr in next st. *1 htr in each of next 6 sts, 2 htr in next st; rep from * to end, ss in top of first 2-ch to join. (48sts)

Round 8 2 ch, 1 htr in each of next 6 sts, 2 htr in next st. *1 htr in each of next 7 sts, 2 htr in next st; rep from * to end, ss in top of first 2-ch to join. (54sts)
Round 9 2 ch, 1 htr in each of next 7 sts, 2 htr in next st. *1 htr in each of next 8 sts, 2 htr in next st; rep from * to end, ss in top of first 2-ch to join. (60sts)
Increases can be stopped sooner or continued as set for a smaller or larger head size
Rounds 10–16 2 ch, work 1 htr in each st to end, ss in top of first 2-ch to join.
Even rounds can be added or subtracted to adjust length of hat
Round 17 With yarn B, 2 ch, work 1 htr in each st to end, ss in top of first 2-ch to join.
Rounds 18–19 With yarn A, 2 ch, work 1 htr in each st to end, ss in top of first 2-ch to join.
Round 20 With yarn B, 2 ch, work 1 htr in each st to end, ss in top of first 2-ch to join.
Round 21 With yarn B, 2 ch, *fphtr in next st, bphtr in next st; rep from * to end, ss in top of first 2-ch to join.
Fasten off, weave in ends.

Ensure that the starting hole is nearly closed after the first round. If not, pull out and start again with a shorter chain.

The decorative stripes are made as part of the stitch pattern. Be sure to stitch in loose ends when switching colours.

BABY'S BOOTIES

These adorable booties are made in the softest yarn for delicate skin, and in a style that is sure to stay on small feet. The booties are made in the round, starting with the sole. Be sure to use a stitch marker throughout to mark the first stitch of the round.

MATERIALS

Size
To fit a newborn baby

Yarn
Sublime Cashmere Merino Silk DK 50g

x 1 ball

Crochet hook
4mm (G-6 US) hook

Tension
Measure tension after completing the sole of each bootie. The length of the sole should be a minimum of 8.5cm (3¼in).

Notions
4 small buttons

PATTERN

BOOTIES (MAKE 2)
Work 9 ch.
Round 1 Miss 1 ch, dc in each ch to end, 4 dc in last ch. Working down other side of ch, dc in each ch to end, work 4 dc in last ch. (22sts)
Round 2 *Dc in next 7 sts, work (1 dc in next st, 2 dc in next st) twice; rep from * once more. (26sts)
Round 3 *Dc in next 7 sts, work (1 dc in each of next 2 sts, 2 dc in next st) twice; rep from * once more. (30sts)
Round 4 *Dc in next 7 sts, work (1 dc in each of next 3 sts, 2 dc in next st) twice; rep from * once more. (34sts)
Round 5 Working into back loops only, dc in each dc to end. (34sts)
Round 6 Dc in next 7 sts, work (1 dc in each of next 3 sts, dc2tog) twice, dc in next 17 sts. (32sts)
Round 7 Dc in next 7 sts, tr2tog 4 times, dc in next 7 sts, htr in next 10 sts. (28sts)
Round 8 Dc in next 7 sts, tr2tog twice, dc in next 7 sts, htr in next 10 sts, ss in first st to close. (26sts)
Do not fasten off yarn.
First strap: 9 ch, dc in 4th ch from hook and in each of next 5 chs, ss in beg st.
Fasten off.

The button loop at the end of each strap needs to fit snugly around the button. Adjust the size by adding or subtracting chains.

Second strap: Rejoin yarn on other side of bootie at corresponding st (the last dc before the htr sts) and rep instructions for first strap. Fasten off, weave in ends. Attach buttons securely, as shown in picture.

The sole of the bootie is worked in rounds without joining. Be sure to check the measurement of each sole for tension.

BABY'S CARDIGAN

A beautiful cardigan for a very special baby, this project is sure to keep your favourite little one warm and cosy. The clever, simple construction incorporates the sleeves into the body of the cardigan so no seaming is needed, making this a great introductory garment project.

MATERIALS

Size
To fit a baby aged 0–6 (6–12) months

Yarn
Jarol Heritage DK/Berroco Vintage DK 100g

A × 2   **B** × 1 ball

Crochet hook
4mm (G-6 US) hook

Notion
3 buttons, approx 1cm (½in) in diameter

Tension
17 htr per 10cm (4in)

PATTERN

FRONT (MAKE 2)
Using yarn B and 4mm hook, work 22 (25) ch.
Row 1 1 htr into 3rd ch from hook, 1 htr into each ch to end. Turn. 20 (23) sts.
Row 2 2 ch, 1 htr into each st across row. Turn. Change to yarn A and work straight in htr until piece measures 15 (16)cm/6 (6½)in.
Next row: 27(32) ch, 1 htr into 3rd ch from hook, then one htr into each ch to end of ch. 25 (30) sts increased for arm. Work across body stitches. 45 (53) htr
Work straight on these sts until piece measures approx 20 (21)cm/8 (8½) in from hem, ending at arm edge.
Next row: Work across in htr to last 6 (8) sts, 1 dc into next st, turn leaving rem sts unworked for neck opening.
Next row: Sl st across 5 sts, htr to end of row. Work straight until piece measures 24 (25)cm/ 9½ (10)in to shoulder.
Fasten off yarn.

BACK
Using yarn B and 4mm hook, work 43 (47) ch.
Row 1 1 htr into 3rd ch from hook, then 1htr into each ch to end. Turn. 41(45) htr
Row 2 2 ch, work 1htr into each st across row. Turn. Change to yarn A and work straight in htr until piece measures the same as front to one row below armhole.
Fasten off yarn.
Using yarn A, work 25 (30) ch, then work across body stitches in htr, work 27 (32) ch.
NEXT ROW: Work 1htr into 3rd ch from hook, then one htr into each ch to end of ch. 25 (30) sts increased for arm. Work in htr across body stitches, then 1 htr into each ch to end for opposite arm. 50 (60) sts in total increased for arms. 91 (105) htr
Work straight on these sts until piece measures same as front to one row below shoulder.
NEXT ROW: Work across 35 (40) sts. Fasten

off yarn, leaving rem sts unworked.
Fasten yarn to opposite arm edge, work across 35 (40) sts, fasten off yarn, leaving rem 21 (25) sts unworked for neck.

FINISHING
Block all pieces lightly to shape. Sew shoulder seams, then sew up each underarm and side seam.

NECK EDGE
Rejoin yarn A to bottom of right front edge and work evenly in dc up edge, then round neck. At top of left edge, work 5 ch for button loop, then work 4 dc down edge, 5 ch, 4 dc, 5 ch, dc to bottom of left front. Sew buttons to right front, corresponding to the button loops.

CUFFS
Using yarn B, rejoin yarn to cuff and work 2 rows of dc evenly round.
Weave in all ends.

Rows of double crochet in a contrasting colour add a neat finishing touch to the cuffs and cardigan hem.

The sleeves are made as part of the back and front pieces of the cardigan.

WRIST WARMERS

Lacy and pretty yet surprisingly warm, this simple wrist warmer pattern works up quickly, and the softly variegated yarn provides visual appeal. This project is made using the arched mesh stitch (see page 41) and a variation of the picot scallop edging (see page 55), both from the Techniques section. Worked flat, the wrist warmers are then joined along the open edges, leaving a thumb hole open.

MATERIALS

Size
To fit an adult female

Yarn
Rowan Creative Focus 100g

x 2 balls

Crochet hook
5mm (H-8 US) hook

Tension
3.5 pattern repeats per 10cm (4in)

PATTERN

WRIST WARMERS (MAKE 2)
Work 28 ch (loosely).
Row 1 Dc in 2nd ch from hook, 3 ch, miss next ch, 1 tr in next ch, *2 ch, miss next ch, 1 dc in next ch, 2 ch, miss next ch, 1 tr in next ch; rep from * to end, turn.
Row 2 1 ch, 1 dc in first tr, 2 ch, 1 tr in next dc, *2 ch, 1 dc in next tr, 2 ch, 1 tr in next dc; rep from * to end, turn.
Rep row 2 until piece measures 17cm (7in).
Do not fasten off.

TOP EDGING
1 ch, dc in first tr. Work [2 dc, 3 ch, 2 dc] in each 2-ch sp to end, dc in last dc. Do not fasten off.

JOINING, BOTTOM EDGING
Slip stitch join down open sides, leaving 4cm (1½in), or length desired, open for thumb hole. When sides are joined, 2 ch and work htr around entire lower edge of piece.
Fasten off, weave in ends. Wrist warmer can be left as is or turned inside out to hide seam, as desired.

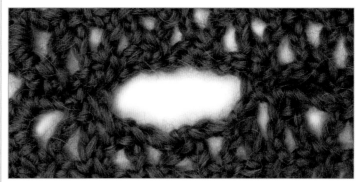

The thumb hole is formed by leaving a gap of around 4cm (1½in) between the two seams when the two sides of the crocheted square are joined together.

Picot edging along the top of each wrist warmer adds a pretty finishing touch.

STRING BAG

Do your part for the environment by making up this surprisingly roomy string bag. It holds more than a typical plastic carrier bag and can be re-used over and over. The bag is made in the round, and has a solid bottom to prevent smaller objects from falling out.

MATERIALS

Size
38cm x 28cm (15in x 11in)

Yarn
Rowan Handknit Cotton 50g

x 2 balls

Crochet hook
4.5mm (7 US) hook

PATTERN

BAG
Work 9 ch.
Join with ss in last ch from hook to form loop.
Round 1 3 ch, 11 tr in loop, ss in top of first 3-ch. (12sts)
Round 2 3 ch, 1 tr in same st. 2 tr in each st to end, ss in top of first 3-ch. (24sts)
Round 3 3 ch, 2 tr in next st. *1 tr in next st, 2 tr in next st; rep from * to end, ss in top of first 3-ch. (36sts)
Round 4 3 ch, 1 tr in next st, 2 tr in next st. *1 tr in each of next 2 sts, 2 tr in next st; rep from * to end, ss in top of first 3-ch. (48sts)
Round 5 3 ch, 1 tr in each of next 2 sts, 2 tr in next st. *1 tr in each of next 3 sts, 2 tr in next st; rep from * to end, ss in top of first 3-ch. (60sts)
Round 6 3 ch, 1 tr in each of next 3 sts, 2 tr in next st. *1 tr in each of next 4 sts, 2 tr in next st; rep from * to end, ss in top of first 3-ch. (72sts)
Round 7 3 ch, 1 tr in each of next 4 sts, 2 tr in next st. *1 tr in each of next 5 sts, 2 tr in next st; rep from * to end, ss in top of first 3-ch. (84sts)
Round 8 *4 ch, miss 2 sts, dc in next st; rep from * to end, omit last dc, end with a ss at base of first 4-ch. (28 4-ch loops)
Round 9 Ss in next 2 chs, *4 ch, dc in next 4-ch loop; rep from * to end, ending ss in first ss from beg of round.
Rounds 10–14 Rep round 9.
Round 15 Ss in next 2 chs, *6 ch, dc in next 4-ch loop; rep from * to end, ending ss in first ss from beg of round.

Round 16 Ss in next 3 chs, *6 ch, dc in next 6-ch loop; rep from * to end, ending ss in first ss from beg of round.
Rounds 17–21 Rep round 16.
Round 22 Ss in next 3 chs, *4 ch, dc in next 6-ch loop; rep from * to end, ending ss in first ss from beg of round.
Rounds 23–27 Rep round 9.
Round 28 *2 ch, dc in next 4-ch loop; rep from * to end, ss at base of first 2-ch loop.

TOP
Round 29 1 ch, *2 dc in next 2-ch loop, dc in next dc; rep from * to end, ss in first 1-ch to join. (82sts)

CREATE HANDLES
Round 30 1 ch, dc in next 8 sts, 24 ch (handle can be lengthened by adding more chs here, as desired), miss 23 sts, dc in 24th st and next 17 sts, 24 ch (handle can be lengthened by adding more chs here, as desired), miss 23 sts, dc in 24th st and rem 10 sts, ss in first st to join.
Round 31 1 ch, dc in same st and in each st to handle, dc in each ch across handle, dc in each st to next handle, dc in each ch across handle, dc to end of round, ss in first st to close.
Round 32 1 ch, dc in same st and in each st all around bag, ss in first st to close.
Fasten off, weave in ends.

Double crochet stitches across the top of the bag give it structure and prevent it from stretching too much when carried.

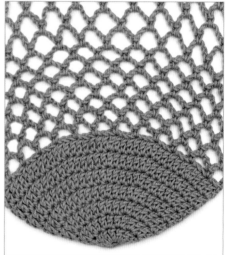

A closed bottom and smaller chain loops in the lower half of the bag ensure that smaller items won't fall out easily.

CLUTCH BAG

This elegant clutch is crocheted in a softly shimmering mercerized cotton and is just big enough to hold all your essentials for an evening out. It is made in rows using the cluster and shell stitch (see page 35) from the Techniques section, and forms its own edging and buttonholes. This is a quick and easy project – why not crochet one for tonight?

MATERIALS

Size
20cm x 10cm (8in x 4in)

Yarn
Rico Essentials Cotton DK/Tahki Cotton Classic 50g

× 1 ball

Crochet hook
3.5mm (E-4 US) hook

Notions
Shell button, approximately 2cm (¾in)

Special notes
Cluster: over next 5 sts, (which include 2 tr, 1 dc, 2 tr), work [yrh and insert hook in next st, yrh and draw a loop through, yrh and draw through first two loops on hook] 5 times (6 loops on hook), yrh and draw through all 6 loops on hook.

PATTERN

Work 46 ch.
Row 1 2 tr in 4th ch from hook, miss next 2 chs, 1 dc in next ch, *miss next 2 chs, 5 tr in next ch, miss next 2 chs, 1 dc in next ch; rep from * to last 3 chs, miss next 2 chs, 3 tr in last ch, turn.
Row 2 1 ch, 1 dc in first tr, *2 ch, 1 cluster over next 5 sts, 2 ch, 1 dc in centre tr of 5-tr group; rep from * to end, working last dc of last rep in top of 3-ch at end, turn.

Row 3 3 ch, 2 tr in first dc, miss next 2 chs, 1 dc in next st (top of first cluster), miss next 2 chs, *5 tr in next dc, miss next 2 chs, 1 dc in next st (top of next cluster); rep from *, ending with 3 tr in last dc, turn. Rep rows 2 and 3 until piece measures 25cm (10in), ending on a row 3. Fold at 10cm (4in) and sew (or use slip stitch join, see page 51) 2 sides to form pocket. Fold top flap over and attach button.

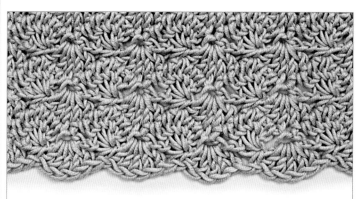

The cluster and shell stitch pattern forms its own decorative edge so there is no need to add edging.

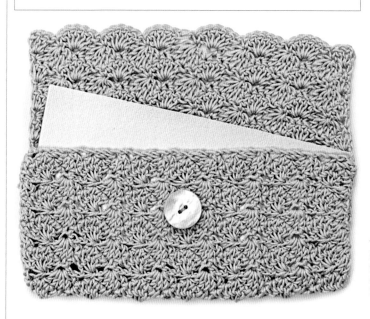

You may choose to line your clutch with fabric, or place a piece of card inside to help it keep its shape.

ROUND CUSHION

Concentric stripes in harmonious shades feature on this pretty cushion. Two flat circles are worked in the round and then sewn together at the edges. This is a quick project that works up easily, and is great for using up leftover lengths of yarn!

MATERIALS

Size
35cm (14in) diameter

Yarn
Debbie Bliss Cashmerino Aran 50g

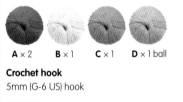

A × 2   **B** × 1   **C** × 1   **D** × 1 ball

Crochet hook
5mm (G-6 US) hook

Notion
Round cushion pad, 35cm (14in) diameter

PATTERN

CUSHION FRONT
With yarn A, work 4 ch, 12 tr in 4th ch from hook, ss in first st to join. (12sts)
Round 1 3 ch, tr in same st. *2 tr in next st; rep from * around, ss in top of first 3-ch to join. (24sts)
Round 2 3 ch, 2 tr in next st. *1 tr in next st, 2 tr in next st; rep from * around, ss in top of first 3-ch to join. (36sts)
Change to yarn B.
Round 3 3 ch, 1 tr in next st, 2 tr in next st. *1 tr in each of next 2 sts, 2 tr in next st; rep from * around, ss in top of first 3-ch to join. (48sts)
Change to yarn C.
Round 4 3 ch, 1 tr in each of next 2 sts, 2 tr in next st. *1 tr in each of next 3 sts, 2 tr in next st; rep from * around, ss in top of first 3-ch to join. (60sts)
Change to yarn D.
Round 5 3 ch, 1 tr in each of next 3 sts, 2 tr in next st. *1 tr in each of next 4 sts, 2 tr in next st; rep from * around, ss in top of first 3-ch to join. (72sts)

Change to yarn A.
Round 6 3 ch, 1 tr in each of next 4 sts, 2 tr in next st. *1 tr in each of next 5 sts, 2 tr in next st; rep from * around, ss in top of first 3-ch to join. (84sts)
Change to yarn B.
Continue in this way, working one additional single tr between increases per round and changing colour in this order every round, to 132 sts, ending with yarn B.
Work one further round in pattern in yarn B. (144sts)
Fasten off yarn.

CUSHION BACK
Work one more cushion side in the same way, but worked entirely in yarn A.

FINISHING
Block pieces lightly (see page 50).
Sew together two pieces around circumference, trapping cushion pad inside.

The treble crochet stitch used for the cover forms a pretty, lacy pattern, showing a glimpse of the cushion underneath.

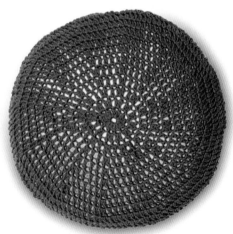

The back of the cushion is worked using the same pattern as on the front, but in a single colour.

CHEVRON CUSHION

A great introduction to colourwork, this moderately easy project uses the zigzag stitch. The entire cushion cover is made in one piece and then stitched up the sides. The buttonholes are created as part of the pattern.

MATERIALS

Size
40cm × 30cm (16in × 12in)

Yarn
A: Sirdar Click DK/Plymouth Yarn Encore 50g
B: Sirdar Country Style/Berroco Vintage DK 50g

A × 2   **B** × 1 ball

Crochet hook
4mm (G-6 US) hook

Notions
Cushion pad 40cm x 30cm/16in x 12in
(or size required for your cushion cover)
5 buttons, approx 1.5cm (½in) in diameter

PATTERN

CUSHION
With yarn B, work 81 ch.
Row 1 1 dc in 2nd ch from hook, 1 dc in each ch to end, turn. (80sts)
Rows 2–3 1 ch, 2 dc in next st, 1 dc in each of next 7 sts, miss next 2 dc, 1 dc in each of next 7 sts, *2 dc in each of next 2 sts, 1 dc in each of next 7 sts, miss next 2 dc, 1 dc in each of next 7 sts; rep from * to last st, 2 dc in last st. Turn. Change to yarn A.
Rows 4–6 2 ch, 2 htr in next st, 1 htr in each of next 7 sts, miss next 2 sts, 1 htr in each of next 7 sts, *2 htr in each of next 2 sts, 1 htr in each of next 7 sts, miss next 2 dc, 1 htr in each of next 7sts; rep from * to last st, 2 htr in last st. Turn. Change to yarn B.
Row 7 1 ch, 2 dc in next st, 1 dc in each of next 7 sts, miss next 2 dc, 1 dc in each of next 7 sts, *2 dc in each of next 2 sts, 1 dc in each of next 7 sts, miss next 2 dc, 1 dc in each of next 7 sts; rep from * to last st, 2 dc in last st. Turn. Change to yarn A.
Rep last 4 rows until work measures approximately 70cm (28in), or desired length – long enough to fit comfortably around a cushion with an overlap.
End with a row 7, then rep row 7 twice more in yarn B.
Fasten off.

FINISHING
Block piece lightly to shape (see page 50). Wrap piece around cushion pad, with an overlap halfway down back of pad. Ensure top edge of piece, with 5 complete points, is on top, overlapping bottom of piece. Sew up bottom two side seams of cushion, then sew down top two side seams, overlapping bottom seam. Fasten middle flap of cushion by sewing buttons on bottom edge of piece, corresponding to first decrease hole in yarn A htr row next to end of each point. Fasten buttons and weave in all ends.

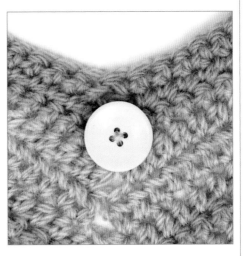

Buttons are fixed to the bottom layer of the cushion cover at the bottom of each "V" in the zigzag pattern.

The stitch pattern forms a neat zigzag edge to the cushion cover. The buttons are simply pushed through holes in the pattern.

PATCHWORK BLANKET

This beautiful blanket is made up of individual squares, which are then joined together and finished with a border. The squares can be crocheted all at once or over time, and the size of the blanket can easily be varied by increasing or decreasing the number of squares in each row or column.

MATERIALS

Size
110cm x 94cm (43in x 37in)

Yarn
Stylecraft Special DK/Red Heart Super Saver Solids®
100g

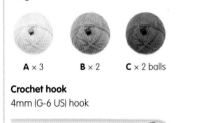

A × 3   **B** × 2   **C** × 2 balls

Crochet hook
4mm (G-6 US) hook

PATTERN

SQUARE

With yarn A, work 4 ch, ss in first ch to form loop.
Round 1 3 ch, 2 tr in loop, *2 ch, 3 tr in loop, rep from * twice more, 2 ch, ss in top of beg 3-ch to join.
Fasten off yarn A.
Round 2 Join yarn B in any centre tr from 3-tr set from prev round. 3 ch, *1 tr in each tr to corner sp. Work (2 tr, 4 ch, 2 tr) in next 2-ch corner sp; rep from * to end, work 1 tr in each rem tr, ss in top of beg 3-ch to join. (7 tr per side of square)
Round 3 3 ch, *1 tr in each tr to corner. Work (2 tr, 4 ch, 2 tr) in 4-ch corner sp. Rep from * to end, work 1 tr in each rem tr, ss in top of beg 3-ch to join. (11 tr per side of square)
Fasten off yarn B.
Round 4 Join yarn A in any tr st. Rep round 3 with yarn A. (15 tr per side of square)
Fasten off yarn A.
Make 27 more squares using yarn B in rounds 2 and 3 (28 B squares total), and 28 squares using yarn C in rounds 2 and 3.

JOIN SQUARES

Lay two squares right sides facing. Work dc join in back loops only of each st. Join squares into strips of 8 squares. Lay two strips of 8 right sides facing. Work dc join in back loops only of each st. Continue until all squares are joined. Sample blanket uses 7 x 8 squares.

EDGING

Round 1 Join yarn A in any tr. 3 ch, *1 tr in each tr to corner sp. Work (2 tr, 4 ch, 2 tr) into each 4-ch corner sp. Rep from * around entire blanket, work 1 tr in each rem tr, ss in top of beg 3-ch to join.
Round 2 Rep round 1.
Fasten off. Weave in all ends.

The squares of the blanket are joined by working through only the back loops of each stitch. This helps the blanket lie flat.

Alternate block colours as shown, or add others to create your own colour combinations.

GRANNY-FLOWER BLANKET

This vibrant update of the vintage-inspired granny-square blanket is crocheted together, not sewn, so it looks great from either side with no obvious seams.
It is perfect for draping over a chair or laying on a single bed.

MATERIALS

Size
Each flower motif measures approx 8cm (3¼in) in diameter. Final blanket measurements are approx 80cm x 120cm (90cm x 170cm, 100cm x190cm)

Yarn
For border: 4 balls of Sirdar Snuggly DK 50g in White (251)
For the flower motifs: use oddments of DK yarn
We used 1 ball of each shade.

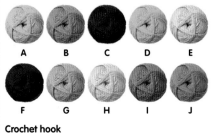

A   B   C   D   E

F   G   H   I   J

Crochet hook
4mm (G-6 US) hook
Yarn needle for darning ends

Tension
Exact tension is not essential for this project.

Special stitches
Puff – (Yrh, insert hook into st, yrh and pull through a lp, drawing it up to the height of a htr) 4 times, 9lps on hook, yrh and pull through all lps on hook.

Popcorn – Work 5tr into next st, remove hook from final stitch, insert it into first of 5tr, then back through last loop, yrh and pull through everything on hook.

PATTERN

MAKING THE FLOWER MOTIFS
Round 1 Using any contrast shade, work 3 ch to count as first tr, work 1 tr into 3rd ch from hook, then work 10 further tr into same chain. Join round with a ss.
Change colour.
Round 2 2 ch, work 1 puff into first tr, 1 ch, (1 puff, 1ch) to end of round, join round with a ss.
Change colour.
Round 3 3 ch, work popcorn into bottom of chain, 3 ch, *work popcorn into next 1-ch sp, 3 ch; rep from * to end of round, join round with ss.

Make enough flower motifs in the same way for the desired size of blanket. For a small blanket, work 96 flowers, for a medium blanket, work 153 flowers, for a large blanket work 190 flowers.

JOINING THE MOTIFS
Using the border shade, work a final row around one flower motif as follows:
Join yarn to any 3-ch sp.
3 ch, (1 tr, 3 ch, 2 tr) all into same sp, *([2 tr, 1 ch, 2 tr] into next 3-ch sp) twice, (2 tr, 3 ch, 2 tr) into next 3-ch sp; rep from * twice more, ([2 tr, 1 ch, 2 tr] into next 3-ch sp) twice, join round with a ss.
To join the next flower to first, finished motif, work border round next flower as follows:
Using the border shade, join yarn to any 3-ch sp.
3 ch, (1 tr, 3 ch, 2 tr) all into same sp, *([2 tr, 1 ch, 2 tr] into next 3-ch sp) twice, 2 tr, 1 ch into next 3 ch sp, work a ss into the central ch of any 3 ch corner sp of first motif to join the corners, 1 ch, 2 tr back into original 3-ch sp of second motif. *2 tr into next 3-ch sp, ss into next 1-ch sp of first motif, 2 tr back into original 3-ch sp of second motif; rep from * once more, 2 tr, 1 ch into next 3-ch sp, ss into central ch of next corner ch of first motif,

1 ch, 2 tr back into original 3-ch sp of second motif, ([2 tr, 1 ch, 2 tr] into next 3-ch sp) twice, (2 tr, 3 ch, 2 tr) into next 3-ch sp, ([2 tr, 1 ch, 2 tr] into next 3-ch sp) twice, join round with a ss.
Work all following motifs from first row in the same way as this, joining each subsequent flower to the previous motif along one side.
On the second row of motifs, join first flower of the row to the motif below in the same way as previously stated. For all following motifs, join along two sides to the motifs immediately adjacent and below it in the same way as before.

For a small blanket arrange 8 motifs wide by 12 motifs long.
For a medium blanket, arrange 9 motifs wide by 17 motifs long.
For a large blanket, arrange 10 motifs wide by 19 motifs long.

FINISHING THE BLANKET
Using the border shade, join yarn to any 3-ch sp.
Work a border round the blanket as follows:
Using the border shade, attach yarn to any corner of blanket.
3 ch, 4 tr into same corner sp, ** *([2 tr, 1 ch, 2 tr] all into next 1-ch sp,) twice, (2 tr, 1 ch, 2 tr) into next joining sp of two motifs; rep from * to next corner of blanket, 5tr into corner sp. ** Rep between ** and ** around entire perimeter, joining round with a ss.

Weave in all ends and block very lightly to shape, being careful not to flatten the 3D nature of the flower motifs.

Crochet flowers without borders make excellent embellishments for hats and scarves, or as brooches with a safety pin sewn on the back. We've used DK weight yarn here, but you could try varying the weights of yarn to make larger and smaller blooms.

BABY'S BLANKET

This adorable baby blanket is made as a large Afghan (or Granny) square with a centre of mini squares and finished with a shell edging. Each new colour is joined directly to the previous square or round, so no seaming is required – just weave in the ends to finish.

MATERIALS

Size
84cm x 84cm (33in x 33in)

Yarn
Sirdar Wash 'n' Wear DK Double Crepe/Borroco Comfort DK 100g

A × 3   **B** × 3 balls

Crochet hook
4mm (G-6 US) hook

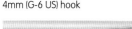

PATTERN

STARTING MINI SQUARE
With yarn A, work 4 ch, ss to first ch to form loop.
Round 1 3 ch, 2 tr in loop. *2 ch, 3 tr in loop; rep from * twice more, 2 ch, ss in top of beg 3-ch to join.
Fasten off.
For next mini square, use the join-as-you-go-method.
With yarn B, work 4 ch, ss to first ch to form loop.
Round 1 3 ch, 2 tr in loop. *dc in any 2-ch corner sp of starting mini square, 3 tr in loop of current square; rep from * once more. 2 ch, 3 tr in loop, 2 ch, ss in top of beg 3-ch to join.
Fasten off.
Continue making and joining the mini squares as you go, alternating colours, until centre large square is desired size. Sample blanket uses 6 x 6 mini squares.

BEGIN GRANNY SQUARE ROUNDS
Join yarn A in next ch sp after any corner.
Round 1 3 ch, 2 tr into same space. *1 ch, 3 tr into next ch sp; rep from * to corner, work (3 tr, 2 ch, 3 tr) in corner space.
Rep around piece. Fasten off yarn A.
Rounds 2–3 Attach yarn B and rep round 1. At the end of round 2, ss in top of beg 3-ch, ss in each st to next ch sp from prev round, then begin as round 1. Fasten off yarn B.
Round 4 Attach yarn A and rep round 1.
Rep rounds 1–3 to form pattern, one round of yarn A and two rounds of yarn B.

Continue with Granny rounds until blanket is desired size. Sample blanket uses 24 rounds, ending on a round 3.

EDGING
Round 1 Attach yarn B in any st. Dc in each st and ch around blanket, working 3 dc in each corner sp. Ss in first dc to join. Fasten off yarn B.
Round 2 Attach yarn A. 2 ch, *5 tr in next dc, dc into next dc. Rep from * around blanket. Fasten off.

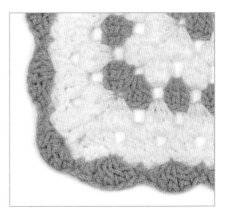

The outermost stripe in this design is actually shell edging. It finishes the blanket without breaking up the pattern of stripes.

A central block of mini squares is surrounded by rounds of traditional Afghan (or Granny) square stitch.

TOY BALLS

These colourful little balls are made with small amounts of 4-ply mercerized cotton, and are a great way to use up leftover yarn. This project uses an especially small hook to achieve a tight tension, essential for making a solid fabric that will hold in the filling.

MATERIALS

Size
5cm (2in) diameter

Yarn
Rowan Siena 4-ply 50g

A × 1   B × 1   C × 1 ball

Crochet hook
2mm (B-1 US) hook

Notions
Toy stuffing

PATTERN

CENTRE STRIPED BALL
With yarn C, make 6 dc in loop (see page 57). Pull tail to close.
Round 1 2 dc in each dc to end. (12sts)
Round 2 *1 dc in next dc, 2 dc in next dc; rep from * to end. (18sts)
Round 3 *1 dc in each of next 2 dc, 2 dc in next dc; rep from * to end. (24sts)
Round 4 *1 dc in each of next 3 dc, 2 dc in next dc; rep from * to end. (30sts)
Round 5 *1 dc in each of next 4 dc, 2 dc in next dc; rep from * to end. (36sts)
Round 6 *1 dc in each of next 5 dc, 2 dc in next dc; rep from * to end. (42sts)
Round 7 *1 dc in each of next 6 dc, 2 dc in next dc; rep from * to end. (48sts)
Rounds 8–9 1 dc in each dc to end, finish last dc with yarn A.
Round 10 With yarn A, work 1 dc in each dc to end, finish last dc with yarn B.
Rounds 11–12 With yarn B, work 1 dc in each dc to end, finish last dc of round 12 with yarn A.
Round 13 With yarn A, work 1 dc in each dc to end, finish last dc with yarn C.
Rounds 14–15 With yarn C, work 1 dc in each dc to end.
Round 16 *1 dc in each of next 6 dc, dc2tog; rep from * to end. (42sts)
Round 17 *1 dc in each of next 5 dc, dc2tog; rep from * to end. (36sts)
Round 18 *1 dc in each of next 4 dc, dc2tog; rep from * to end. (30sts)
Round 19 *1 dc in each of next 3 dc, dc2tog; rep from * to end. (24sts)
Round 20 *1 dc in each of next 2 dc, dc2tog; rep from * to end. (18sts)
Round 21 *1 dc in next dc, dc2tog; rep from * to end. (12sts)
Stuff very firmly.
Round 22 dc2tog to end. (6sts)
Fasten off, leaving a long tail. Use tail to close hole, weave in ends.

ALL-OVER STRIPED BALL
Follow above pattern, but change the yarn colour in each round, finishing the last st of prev round with new colour.

TRICOLOURED BLOCK BALL
With yarn B, make 6 dc in loop (see page 57). Pull tail to close.
Round 1 2 dc in each dc to end. (12sts)
Round 2 *1 dc in next dc, 2 dc in next dc; rep from * to end. (18sts)
Round 3 *1 dc in each of next 2 dc, 2 dc in next dc; rep from * to end. (24sts)

Round 4 *1 dc in each of next 3 dc, 2 dc in next dc; rep from * to end. (30sts)
Round 5 *1 dc in each of next 4 dc, 2 dc in next dc; rep from * to end. (36sts)
Round 6 *1 dc in each of next 5 dc, 2 dc in next dc; rep from * to end. (42sts)
Round 7 *1 dc in each of next 6 dc, 2 dc in next dc; rep from * to end, finish last st with yarn A. (48sts)
Rounds 8–15 With yarn A, work 1 dc in each dc to end, finish last st of round 15 with yarn C.
Round 16 With yarn C, *1 dc in each of next 6 dc, dc2tog; rep from * to end. (42sts)
Round 17 *1 dc in each of next 5 dc, dc2tog; rep from * to end. (36sts)
Round 18 *1 dc in each of next 4 dc, dc2tog; rep from * to end. (30sts)
Round 19 *1 dc in each of next 3 dc, dc2tog; rep from * to end. (24sts)
Round 20 *1 dc in each of next 2 dc, dc2tog; rep from * to end. (18sts)
Round 21 *1 dc in next dc, dc2tog; rep from * to end. (12sts)
Stuff very firmly.
Round 22 dc2tog to end. (6sts)
Fasten off, leaving a long tail. Use tail to close hole, weave in ends.

The starting and end points of the different coloured rounds form an off-set seam down the back of the ball.

BOOKMARK

Worked in fine crochet cotton, this small project makes a lovely and quick gift. If you have never used crochet cotton and a small hook before, a bit of care and patience is required but the results are stunning. Press the bookmark lightly once finished to flatten it.

MATERIALS

Size
2cm x 18cm (¾in x 7in)

Yarn
DMC Petra 100g

× 1 ball

Crochet hook
1.5mm (6 steel US) hook

PATTERN

BOOKMARK
Work 51 ch.
Row 1 Miss 1 ch, dc in each rem ch to end. (50sts)
Rows 2–3 1 ch, turn. Dc in each dc to end. (50sts)
Row 4 1 ch, turn. Dc in first st, *miss 1 st, 5 tr in next st, miss 1 st, ss in next st; rep from * around entire piece including other side of foundation chain, ending dc in last st, leaving last short side unworked. Fasten off, weave in ends.

TASSEL
Cut 8 lengths of cotton twice the length of desired tassel (sample used lengths of 40cm/16in). Insert hook into centre of unworked short side, fold cotton lengths over hook at centre of lengths, pull loop through, fold all tails over hook and pull tails through. Trim neatly.

A tassel is surprisingly easy to make. It provides a neat finishing touch and makes it easy to find your place in the book.

Shell edging runs along both sides of the bookmark, giving the appearance of a symmetrical pattern.

TEDDY BEAR

This adorable teddy is made in continuous rounds. The head is started from the top and the body from the bottom; both are decreased to the same number of stitches and then stuffed and joined. Arms, legs, and ears are added separately, as is a contrasting scarf.

MATERIALS

Size
15cm (6in)

Yarn
A (for teddy): Stylecraft Special DK/Red Heart Super Saver Solids® 100g
B (for scarf): Rowan Purelife DK 50g

A × 1   B × 1 ball

Crochet hook
A: 3mm (D-3 US) hook (for teddy)
B: 4mm (G-6 US) hook (for scarf)

A
B

Notions
Toy stuffing
Light brown and black embroidery thread

PATTERN

HEAD
Make 6 dc in loop (see page 57), pull tail to close.
Round 1 2 dc in each dc to end. (12sts)
Round 2 *1 dc in next dc, 2 dc in next dc; rep from * to end. (18sts)
Round 3 *1 dc in each of next 2 dc, 2 dc in next dc; rep from * to end. (24sts)
Round 4 *1 dc in each of next 3 dc, 2 dc in next dc; rep from * to end. (30sts)
Round 5 *1 dc in each of next 4 dc, 2 dc in next dc; rep from * to end. (36sts)
Round 6 *1 dc in each of next 5 dc, 2 dc in next dc; rep from * to end. (42sts)
Rounds 7–14 1 dc in each dc to end. (42sts)
Round 15 *1 dc in each of next 5 dc, dc2tog; rep from * to end. (36sts)
Round 16 *1 dc in each of next 4 dc, dc2tog; rep from * to end. (30sts)
Round 17 *1 dc in each of next 3 dc, dc2tog; rep from * to end. (24sts)
Fasten off, leaving a long tail. Embroider eyes, nose, and mouth. Stuff firmly.

EARS (Make 2)
Make 5 dc in magic loop, pull tail to close.
Round 1 2 dc in each dc to end. (10sts)
Rounds 2–3 1 dc in each dc to end. (10sts)
Fasten off, leaving a long tail. Use tail to sew open ends of ears to head.

BODY
Make 6 dc in magic loop, pull tail to close.
Round 1 2 dc in each dc to end. (12sts)
Round 2 *1 dc in next dc, 2 dc in next dc; rep from * to end. (18sts)
Round 3 *1 dc in each of next 2 dc, 2 dc in next dc; rep from * to end. (24sts)
Round 4 *1 dc in each of next 3 dc, 2 dc in next dc; rep from * to end. (30sts)
Round 5 *1 dc in each of next 4 dc, 2 dc in next dc; rep from * to end. (36sts)
Round 6 *1 dc in each of next 5 dc, 2 dc in next dc; rep from * to end. (42sts)
Rounds 7–14 1 dc in each dc to end. (42sts)
Round 15 *1 dc in each of next 5 dc, dc2tog; rep from * to end. (36sts)
Rounds 16–17 1 dc in each dc to end. (36sts)
Round 18 *1 dc in each of next 4 dc, dc2tog; rep from * to end. (30sts)
Rounds 19–20 1 dc in each dc to end. (30sts)
Round 21 *1 dc in each of next 3 dc, dc2tog; rep from * to end. (24sts)
Rounds 22–23 1 dc in each dc to end. (24sts)
Fasten off, leaving a long tail. Stuff firmly. Sew body to head.

LEGS (Make 2)
Make 6 dc in magic loop, pull tail to close.
Round 1 2 dc in each dc to end. (12sts)
Round 2 *1 dc in next dc, 2 dc in next dc; rep from * to end. (18sts)
Round 3 *1 dc in each of next 2 dc, 2 dc in next dc; rep from * to end. (24sts)
Round 4 *1 dc in each of next 3 dc, 2 dc in next dc; rep from * to end. (30sts)
Round 5 dc2tog to end. (15sts)
Rounds 6–9 1 dc in each dc to end. (15sts)
Fasten off, leaving a long tail. Stuff firmly, use tail to sew legs to body.

ARMS (Make 2)
Make 6 dc in magic loop, pull tail to close.
Round 1 2 dc in each dc to end. (12sts)
Rounds 2–8 1 dc in each dc to end. (12sts)
Fasten off, leaving a long tail. Stuff firmly, use tail to sew arms to body.

SCARF
Work 31 ch.
Row 1 Miss 1 dc, dc in rem 30 chs. (30sts)
Row 2 1 ch, dc in each dc to end.
Fasten off, weave in ends.

The head and neck are both worked to the same number of stitches, and attached to each other with matching yarn.

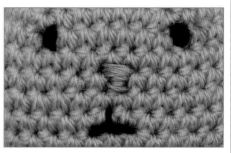

The teddy's eyes, nose, and mouth are embroidered on the finished head with black and light brown embroidery thread.

Index

ABOUT THE AUTHORS

Sally Harding, author of the Tools and Materials and Techniques sections, is a needlecraft technician, author, designer, and editor. Born in the United States, she now lives in London. She was the Technical Knitting Editor for Vogue *Knitting* from 1982, and has for many years edited needlecraft books by acclaimed textile designer Kaffe Fassett. Her books include Crochet Style (1987), *Fast Knits Fat Needles* (2005), and Quick Crochet Huge Hooks (2005).

Catherine Hirst, designed and created the following projects: Beanie hat, Wrist warmers, Lacy scarf, Shawl, Baby booties, Toy balls, Teddy bear, Bookmark, String bag, Clutch bag, and Project basket. Catherine is a professional textiles and crafts instructor at colleges and independent studios across London, the UK, and abroad. She teaches knitting, crochet, and hand embroidery to groups and individuals at all levels. Her work has been featured in top craft publications, including *Mollie Makes*, *Let's Knit*, *Inside Crochet*, *Handmade Living*, *Simply Crochet*, and *Crafts Beautiful*. Catherine is the author of *Teeny Tiny Crochet* (2012) and *Granny Square Crochet* (2012). Visit her at www.catherinehirst.com.

Claire Montgomerie, designed and created the Baby's cardigan, Round cushion, Granny-flower blanket, and Chevron cushion. Claire is a textiles designer who specializes in knitting and crochet, constructing fabrics, garments, creatures, and accessories that are fun, quirky and modern. Her main aim is to reinvent the products of ancient and traditional needlecraft processes, while retaining all their intricacies and comforting charm. Claire has written many knitting and crochet books and also edits the UK craft magazine, *Inside Crochet*.
Find out more at www.montyknits.blogspot.com.

Erin McCarthy, designed and created the Baby's blanket and Patchwork blanket. Erin learned to crochet three years ago after longing to make beautiful crocheted blankets like those she had spied all over blogland. Crochet acts as a relaxing hobby that balances out a busy day job as a special needs teacher. Erin would like to thank Catherine Hirst for teaching her everything she knows about crochet!

ACKNOWLEDGMENTS

Dorling Kindersley would like to thank:
Tia Sarkar for editorial assistance; Ria Holland for design assistance; Jenny Latham for proofreading; Marie Lorimer for indexing; Coral Mula for the crochet diagrams; Lana Pura, Willow Fabrics, House of Smocking and The Contented Cat for materials, equipment, and resources; Usha International for sewing machines.

Creative technicians:
Arijit Ganguly, Archana Singh, Amini Hazarika, Bani Ahuja, Chanda Arora, Christelle Weinsberg, Eleanor Van Zandt, Evelin Kasikov, Geeta Sikand, Indira Sikand, Kusum Sharma, Medha Kshirsagar, Meenal Gupta, Nandita Talukder, Nalini Barua, Neerja Rawat, Resham Bhattacharjee, Rose Sharp Jones, Suchismita Banerjee. Special thanks to Bishnu Sahoo, Vijay Kumar, Rajesh Gulati, Tarun Sharma, Sanjay Sharma.